RETHINKING RELIGION

A CONCISE INTRODUCTION

WILL DEMING

New York / Oxford
OXFORD UNIVERSITY PRESS
2005

Oxford University Press

Oxford   New York
Auckland   Bangkok   Buenos Aires   Cape Town   Chennai
Dar es Salaam   Delhi   Hong Kong   Istanbul   Karachi   Kolkata
Kuala Lumpar   Madrid   Melbourne   Mexico City   Mumbai
Nairobi   São Paulo   Shanghai   Taipei   Tokyo   Toronto

Copyright © 2005 by Oxford University Press, Inc.

Published by Oxford University Press, Inc.
198 Madison Avenue, New York, New York 10016
http://www.oup.com

Oxford is a registered trademark of Oxford University Press

Library of Congress Cataloging-in-Publication Data

Deming, Will, 1956–
    Rethinking religion : a concise introduction / by Will Deming.
        p. cm.
    Includes bibliographical references (p.) and index.
    ISBN 0-19-516981-6 (paper)—ISBN 0-19-516980-8 (cloth)
        1. Religion—Textbooks.   I. Title.

BL48.D387 2004
200–dc22
                                                                2004047312

Printing number: 9 8 7 6 5 4 3 2 1

Printed in the United States of America
on acid-free paper

RETHINKING RELIGION

For Wendy Doniger and Frank Reynolds

CONTENTS

PREFACE

The opportunity to finish the initial draft of this book came during a sabbatical leave in the fall of 2001. In the shadow of the religiously inspired terrorist attacks by Osama bin Laden and his Al-Qaeda network on September 11, its completion took on new relevance. Overnight, Americans had rediscovered religion:

- Terms like "evil" reentered the vocabulary of public discourse.
- "God bless America" was again politically correct.
- Religious leaders of all stripes redoubled efforts at interfaith dialogue.
- Even the initial response from the U.S. government bore a religious stamp: Operation Infinite Justice.

Islam especially became a focal point. Bookstores reported empty shelves regarding all things Muslim, and churches and civic groups around the country competed for Muslim speakers.

While these are encouraging developments, they also highlight the inadequacy of our educational system and popular media in fathoming religion, for it is not as though religion has just now become important to the lives of Americans. It was, in part, the fanatical devotion of Japanese soldiers to a divine emperor that argued for the dropping of two atomic bombs on Japan in 1945—an action of such enormity that it has never been repeated. Three years later, the Jewish hope of reestablishing the biblical nation of Israel became a reality, setting the stage for U.S. involvement in a protracted Middle East conflict. By 1950 two of the world's three superpowers, China and the former Soviet Union, were controlled by explicitly *anti*-religious regimes. Since the sixties evangelical and conservative Christians have been an important factor in U.S. politics, while Islamic nationalism has been on the rise in eastern Europe and southern Asia.

The seventies witnessed an explosive synthesis of Marxism and "liberation theology" in Latin America, and in 1979 the Ayatollah Khomeini established a theocracy in Iran amid anti-American, apocalyptic expectations. More recently, the names Salman Rushdie, Aum Shinrikyo, David Koresh, Heaven's Gate, Hamas, and Shiite have become household words, while India, the world's second most populous nation, elected its first head of state from the ranks of its religiously "untouchables." When we then consider that almost 20 percent of the world's population is Muslim, and that Islam is the fastest growing religion in many parts of the world, it is all the more surprising that September 11 exposed Americans as so uninformed.

As one who has taught college-level introductions to religion for the past eleven years, I felt almost compelled to write this book. Several years ago I noticed a discrepancy between what my freshmen were learning and what I was hearing on the news. One incident that made me sit up and take notice was an interview on National Public Radio in which an incredulous anchor, Bob Edwards, asked a reporter in Bosnia how it was that starving Muslim refugees refused to eat U.S. military rations simply because they contained pork. (Muslims, like Jews, consider pork defiling.)

A few years later, in 1996, my university and *Commonweal* magazine sponsored a symposium entitled "Religion and the Media," inviting senior writers from the *New York Times*, *U.S. News and World Report*, and *Newsweek*. I went to this symposium with high expectations, but they were soon dashed as each speaker proceeded to talk about the media and *his* or *her* religion. There was no discussion of the media's role in public discourse on religion per se, only a call for better coverage of the particular religious viewpoints of the speakers themselves.

The straws that broke the camel's back came in December 1996, and April 1997, when *Time* magazine and the *Washington Post*, respectively, printed photographs of religious texts upside down. Clearly the mainstream media are not always familiar with even the basic data of religions. Because of these experiences, the necessity of writing this book pressed itself upon me until five years ago, when I began the first chapter.

In the last years of writing, it has also become clear to me that I have wanted to write this book for a long time. At the Sidwell Friends School in Washington, DC, I was privileged to take American history with the late Roderick Cox. Through his teaching I became fascinated with theories that purported to explain human motivations in history. By graduation I had been introduced to economic theory and eventually chose to major in economics at the College of William and Mary.

It was at college that I became a Christian and took my first course in South Asian religions. Religious motivations, I began to learn, had inspired many of the achievements of human civilization. Mathematics, literature, law, astronomy, drama, and philosophy all have their beginnings in religion, and before the modern era there was little "art for art's sake." In many ways, then, "human history is essentially the history of religion."[1] My discovery, moreover, was not that this ought to be so, but that it is so, and if one wants to understand human motivations, one needs, among other things, to understand religion.

By graduation I had decided to continue my study of religion at the University of Chicago, where I had the very good fortune of having Wendy Doniger and Frank Reynolds as principal teachers. It is to these two persons, for their guidance into mythology, symbolism, the history of religions, and comparative religious ethics, that I dedicate the present work.

For their instruction and encouragement during the early incubation of this book I also give my thanks to Lee MacVaugh, Jack Van Horn, and the late Harvey K. LeSure.

Beyond this, I express my gratitude to my students at the University of Portland; to all the gracious people at the various temples, synagogues, churches, and mosques I visited, for their patience and insights; and to the following persons for reading drafts and helping me think through this book: Matthew Baasten; Tom Hosinski, C.S.C.; Dan Danner; Jim Moore; Gary Malecha; Elise Moentmann; Khalid Khan; Wm. B. Hund, C.S.C.; Jim Connelly, C.S.C.; Franz Mayr; John Kurtzke, C.S.C.; Mark Utlaut; Deborah MacKinnon; Leonard Houx; Forrest Wheeler; Ken Brown; Blair and Kathy Boone; Norma Bradfish; Catherine Rutledge-Gorman; Dale Hess; Steve Maling; Ann van Bever; Lynn Barlow; Mary Weaver; and my father, Andrew S. Deming.

Finally, I wish to thank my wife, Lauren Wellford Deming, who read every sentence of every draft and provided me with many thoughtful comments; my mother, Maidee Elizabeth Coffman Deming, whose idea it was to add pictures, illustrations, and boxed quotations to the manuscript; my colleague and friend Richard Rutherford, C.S.C., for our extended conversations over this book; and my editor Robert Miller, his assistant Emily Voigt, and the several reviewers who provided criticisms of the manuscript for Oxford University Press and Longman.

RETHINKING RELIGION

INTRODUCTION

The purpose of this book is to demystify religion. Especially in the last century, people in the West have prided themselves on being able to reckon with the world openly, critically, and analytically. Yet most Westerners still find it difficult to come to terms with religion in this way. Seen as the domain of the individual, the insider, or the devout, religion is rarely the object of neutral inquiry, especially in the public square. By "demystifying" religion, then, I mean making it more accessible to Western analytical thinking.

As a concise introduction, the book presents a panorama of the issues important to the analysis of religion. Part one, Starting Points, provides the basis for an analytical approach. It makes the initial case for studying religion in this manner (chapter 1), supplies the reader with a definition of religion (chapter 2), and examines the important role "symbols" play in religions (chapter 3).

In this book, we will define religion as an action: "orientation to ultimate reality." This has the advantage of moving us beyond the vague and mostly unproductive notions of religion as "belief," "faith," or "tradition." It also makes possible a neutral, descriptive approach to our subject, for it allows us to work with the data of religions without having to affirm or deny the validity of any particular religion. Whether or not there is an ultimate reality and whether or not one particular religion is more true than another are matters we will leave to the end of the book.

Part two (chapters 4–9) is entitled Thirty Examples. It offers models for the analysis of religion from six traditions: Hinduism, Buddhism, Judaism, Christianity, Islam, and primal religions.

Part three, Complexities, Limits, Ethics, adds a new level of sophistication to our discussion. It considers the impact that historical change can have on religions (chapter 10), several other complications of analysis (chapter 11), the limitations of an analytical approach (chapter 12), and the ethics of studying someone else's religion in this way (chapter 13).

Part four, Comparison and Evaluation, changes the focus of our discussion. It broaches three matters that have fascinated Westerners over the years: the practice of comparing two or more religions (chapter 14), the question of the validity or truth of religion (chapter 15), and the possibilities for preferring one religion over another (chapter 16).

These four parts are followed by a brief conclusion, a postscript on Science and Religions, an analytical glossary, some suggestions for further reading, and an index of subjects.

Interspersed within the text, the reader will find photographs, illustrations, and boxed quotations. The purpose of these materials is to give easy entry into matters that can only be touched on here. The photographs and illustrations offer a window into the everyday sights and objects of religions. The boxed quotations provide the reader with a sense of the discussions about religion that have taken place in the past century. The footnotes to these quotations, along with the suggestions for further reading, supply additional information.

So much for an overview of the book. In the next chapter we will consider why anyone would want to study religion in the first place. The reason I give, if I may anticipate myself, is not because religion is good or that all human beings *ought* to be religious. It is because religions are very much a part of our world, more than most of us realize. While I am a gardener myself, to use the metaphor I develop at the end of chapter 16, I have written this book as a botanist. The argument in these pages is an argument about the way things in our world are and have been, not necessarily the way they *ought* to be.

Part One

Starting Points

chapter 1

WHY STUDY RELIGION?

According to recent estimates, as much as 85 percent of the world's population are adherents of a religious tradition.[1] This means that the overwhelming majority of people in the world are, to some extent, motivated by specifically religious concerns. Thus the study of religion can provide insight into the hearts, minds, and activities of most of humanity. To the degree that we assign importance to learning foreign languages and understanding other cultures or value the insights of anthropology, sociology, political science, and psychology, the study of religion, too, should be our concern. And this will be true for both the religious and the nonreligious.

> We begin our exploration . . . with the observation that religion is a universal and abiding dimension of human experience.
>
> —*James Livingston*[2]

For the religious, the study of religion can give one a deeper appreciation for his or her own religious tradition, just as a person who has a general understanding of wine is more able to appreciate a particular vintage he or she likes. It also enables a person to articulate his or her tradition better to others, either to edify one's own group or for purposes of evangelism or interfaith dialogue. For both the religious and the nonreligious—the atheist, the agnostic, or the comfortably uninterested—an appreciation of religion gives one insight into dealing with religious people of all sorts. Even detractors of religion will find benefit in this study, just as someone attempting to eliminate a problem, be it AIDS or communism or capitalism, needs first to understand it. Studying religion does not mean becoming religious, no more than studying racism means becoming a racist.

> Religion is the heart of human life.
>
> —*Arnold Toynbee*[3]

> The study of religion is the study of persons.
>
> —*Wilfred Cantwell Smith*[4]

In America, where more religions are practiced than anywhere else in the world, religious people have a voice in many things that affect our day-to-day lives. Here are some examples:

- On the domestic front, religion frequently influences the outcome of political debates on issues such as legalized abortion, gay and lesbian rights, the death penalty, anti-tax initiatives, gene research, the privatization of public services, government funding of the arts, gun control, and doctor-assisted suicide. Groups like the Moral Majority, the Christian Coalition, and the so-called Religious Right have played a significant role in the election of four of our last five presidents—Carter, Reagan, George H.W. Bush, and George W. Bush—the last of whom has proposed a program of "faith-based initiatives" as a way for religion and government to work together.

> For men do strange things under the influence of religion—strange, strange things. . . . There remains so much to be understood.
>
> —*Ninian Smart*[5]

- In popular culture, religion influences even the play of American schoolchildren. "Pocket monsters" called Pokémon, for example, are a Japanese creation that currently animates the imaginations of many of America's pre-teens. Anyone familiar with Japanese religions, however, will recognize the resemblance between these Pokémon and the divine beings of Shinto, known as *kami*. Like Pokémon, *kami* are the elusive source of strange and marvelous apparitions found in forests and other unpopulated areas of the natural world.
- In a more ominous vein, religions can trigger domestic crises:
  The bombing of women's clinics and the murder of doctors who perform abortions
  The violent confrontation in 1993 between federal agents and David Koresh's Branch Davidians in Waco, Texas, which claimed over 80 lives
  The mass suicides of Heaven's Gate, in which 39 took their lives during the 1997 appearance of the Hale-Bopp comet, and of the Peoples' Temple, in which 914 died in 1978
  Acts of terrorism, such as the Al-Qaeda network's 1998 bombing of U.S. embassies in East Africa and its devastating attack of September 11, 2001, on the World Trade Center in New York and the Pentagon in Washington, DC
- Internationally, the United States government has invested considerable resources and political capital to promote peace in the Middle East. While most Americans have some idea of the cultural and political forces that keep the two sides apart, few understand the religious dimensions of the situation. On the Israeli side, many hold that God gave the Jews the land

of Israel. This is an idea found in the Bible, and one that is avidly supported by numerous "friends of Israel" in America. These have included large numbers of conservative Christian voters, as well as nationally prominent politicians and evangelists, like Jimmy Carter, Ronald Reagan, Billy Graham, and Pat Robertson. It is no accident that in 1980 Israel's Prime Minister Menachem Begin honored Christian evangelist Jerry Falwell for his "distinguished service" to the State of Israel, awarding him the prestigious Jabotinsky Centennial Medal. For these Israelis and for many of their supporters, any suggestion that Jews should cease new settlement projects, withdraw from occupied territories, or engage in some other form of a "land-for-peace" agreement is unthinkable. Beyond raising concerns of national security, it is a sin that threatens their relationship with God.

> I've been to Masada. I've toured Judea-Samaria [biblical names for the West Bank]. I've walked the streets of Jerusalem. And I've stood on the Golan Heights. . . . I didn't see any "occupied territory." I saw Israel.
>
> —*Tom DeLay, speaking as House Majority Whip*[6]

On the Palestinian side, which includes not only Palestinians, of course, but also *most* of the Arab world and *much* of the Muslim world, Judaism is understood as an outmoded and corrupt form of monotheism, superseded by Islam. Those who hold this view naturally lack sympathy for the religious concerns of Israelis, and they often resist the very idea of a Jewish nation existing in territory that was formerly Islamic. "For Muslims," as Bernard Lewis writes, "no piece of land once added to the realm of Islam can ever be finally renounced."[7] Consequently, militants among them, who call themselves the Islamic Resistance Movement (Hamas), the Party of God (Hizbullah), the Palestine Islamic Jihad, or the Al-Aqsa Martyrs' Brigade, wage "holy war" against Israelis, an act of devotion to Allah for which they are honored and celebrated in Islamic communities. Thus, it is hardly an exaggeration to say that avowedly *religious* people on both sides have time and again made peace in the region impossible.

> As the nation debates a march toward war in the Middle East, all of us would do well to pay attention to the beliefs of the vast company of Americans who read the headlines and watch the news through a filter of prophetic belief.
>
> —*Paul Boyer, just prior to the 2003 U.S. invasion of Iraq*[8]

- In the world of international business, the vast consumer populations of Asia, Africa, and Central and South America offer marketing opportunities that call for an understanding of the religious sensibilities in those regions. Consider the difficulties encountered by international relief organizations when their efforts to distribute supplies after the January 2001 earthquake in Gujarat, India, were hampered by the survivors' deference to the Hindu caste system. Village leaders insisted on making relief available on the basis not only of need, but also of religious status. Or take the fiasco that erupted later that year when the Japanese-owned subsidiary PT Ajinomoto marketed its pork-based version of MSG (monosodium glutamate) in the predominantly Muslim country of Indonesia: Nearly three thousand *tons* of the flavor enhancer had to be recalled.

Just as they have courted an important kosher clientele in the United States and Europe, corporations seeking to build a consumer base in Islamic countries need to familiarize themselves with Muslim dress codes; restrictions on alcohol, gambling, and pork; and the practices of daily prayer and of fasting during the month of Ramadan. Likewise, those seeking inroads into the markets of India need to identify and cater to Hindu, Muslim, Jain, and Sikh expectations for goods and services. McDonald's, for example, has already established franchises in India that do not serve beef, as cows are sacred among Hindus.[9] As Western industrialization spreads out over the globe, American corporations will do well to remember that Muslims and Hindus make up fully *one-third* of the world's population.

- On the level of corporate management, American executives who maintain ties with businesspeople in other areas of the world are usually more effective when they can empathize with the religious outlook of their foreign counterparts. While such career titles as *The One Minute Manager* and *The 7 Habits of Highly Effective People* have been best-sellers in this country, foreign executives find these books far less useful. In Japan, for example, where corporate culture is deeply influenced by Confucian and Buddhist ideals of success and decorum, business managers have their own list of bestsellers.

> Within an Islamic framework, for example, religion may interconnect the ways in which you eat, make money, raise your children, etc., all specifiable through the single principle of *Tahara*, "ritual purity," which, in Islam, is mainly a matter of maintaining a God-given cosmological order.
>
> —*Jeppe Jensen*[10]

Rather than ask, Why study religion?, the better questions might be: Why have we, as a society, not studied religion *more*? Why is this important topic not regularly addressed in our public education systems until college? And why, more often than not, is the serious study of religion reserved for graduate schools?

Some of the answer lies in our tradition of separating religion and civic life, or "church and state." When this is combined with our culture's inability

> We had 10 or 12 university degrees between us and we . . . could have put all of what we knew about Islam and Muslims in a thimble.
>
> —Ann Fruechte, parish assistant, describing a pastoral meeting at a large metropolitan church[11]

to distinguish clearly between the *study* of religion, on the one hand, and its *practice*, on the other, the public discussion of religion becomes doubly suspect. Simply raising religious concerns in the public square can be seen as promoting a religious position, and carries with it the risk of being marginalized as un-American, a religious fanatic, or both.

It is also true that when Americans think about religion they tend to envision their own: For most people "religion" means only "my religion." This perspective necessarily truncates any appreciation of religion, for, as the adage goes, to know only one of a species is to know none at all. It also inclines people away from *analyzing* religion. From this narrow perspective, the analysis of religion will always seem intrusive: a sterile examination of the things one holds most dear.

Beyond these considerations, the United States is a highly secularized society, with the consequence that religious ways of thinking are looked on as inferior or antithetical to science. Since we often equate "scientific" with "analytical," the very notion of analyzing religion sounds to many like a contradiction in terms. Witness the clumsiness of naming the study of religion "religious science," by analogy with "political science," or calling a student of religion a "religiologist," by analogy with "biologist." While our word "physicist" refers to one studying physics, "religionist" conveys the notion that one is practicing, not studying, religion. In an ideological environment such as this, public discussion of religion will be seldom and brief. While Americans are eager to examine publicly, and in microscopic detail, almost any other aspect of life, including sexual relationships and personal tragedies, we continue to avoid the topic of religion. It is considered a personal matter, best left at home.

This state of affairs has been changing over the last few decades. Organizations like the Pew Charitable Trusts and the Lilly Foundation have sponsored public awareness of the religious dimensions of our world, and the national media now cover the religious beat on a regular basis. Even so, most media coverage still provides only human interest fillers. The pomp and circumstance of religions take center stage, and religious pronouncements are as bland as they are harmless: "The Dalai Lama's wardrobe included a mixture of traditional and western ele-

> It is a feature of a democratic and pluralistic society that our religion is our own business—something we need not even discuss with others.
>
> —Richard Rorty[12]

ments"; "thousands gather as the Pope blesses the faithful and calls for greater understanding between world leaders."[13]

The simplistic nature of this approach is striking. What if the media were to analyze the financial news in this way?—"At dawn, thousands of traders wearing the traditional dark suit and 'power tie' undertook the pilgrimage to Wall Street, the inner sanctum of the financial world. After several mysterious ups and downs in the market, the day came to a close with the ringing of the ceremonial bell." That the popular analysis of religion should lag so far behind the popular analysis of the financial markets is remarkable. Even the public appreciation of music—as evidenced by NPR's "Performance Today," Karl Haas's "Adventures in Good Music," or Peter Schickele's "Schickele Mix"—outstrips the public appreciation of religion. Yet surely the terms "holy," "ritual," and "salvation" are no more esoteric than "arpeggio," "basso continuo," and "aria."

The media's characteristic packaging of religious news also promotes the misguided view that all religious people are of three types: the well-meaning, the dishonest, and the dangerous. In the first instance, religious adherents are portrayed as sincere and benign, their religious traditions essentially all the same and equally irrelevant. Such treatments are generally tempered with expressions of reverence for these good people and their institutions.

The second stereotype is religion as spectacle. Essentially a hoax and a sham, religion caters to the needs of the gullible, who flock to witness the antics of Jimmy Swaggart, Jim and Tammy Bakker, and other televangelists. Third is religion as dangerous menace. Here the focus is on those contemptible "fundamentalists" and "fanatics," who advance their misguided convictions through ignorance, bigotry, and violence. While there is a kernel of truth in almost any stereotype, such treatments provide no insight into the dis-

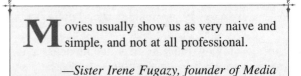

Movies usually show us as very naive and simple, and not at all professional.

—*Sister Irene Fugazy, founder of Media Images and Religious Awareness*[14]

tinctively *religious* significance of religious people. There is a continuum between the persons stereotyped in this way, and dividing them into these stock caricatures only obscures what it means for people to be motivated by religion.

Take the religious use of violence. This is not, as public sentiment would have it, an aberration of religion, but a constant feature in the complete spectrum of religious behavior. A moment's reflection on the Crusades or Islamic "holy wars" shows this to be true historically, and the ongoing conflicts in Northern Ireland (between Catholics and Protestants), Israel and Palestine (between Jews and Muslims), and Sri Lanka (between Hindus and Buddhists), as well as the dramatic rise of militant fundamentalism around the world, should be enough to dispel any notion that religious violence is something the modern world has outgrown. Here I refer specifically to the religious militants in the United States, Japan, China, the Philippines, Malaysia, Indonesia, Sri Lanka, India, Pakistan,

> We've been told they were zealots, fueled by religious fervor—and if you live to be a thousand years old, will that make any sense to you? Will that make any goddamn sense?
>
> —*David Letterman, on the terrorism of September 11, 2001*[15]

Afghanistan, Russia, Kazakhstan, Uzbekistan, Turkmenistan, Tajikistan, Kyrgyzstan, Azerbijan, Georgia, Iraq, Iran, Qatar, United Arab Emirates, Saudi Arabia, Yemen, Israel, Palestine, Jordan, Lebanon, Syria, Turkey, Ethiopia, Sudan, Egypt, Tunisia, Algeria, Nigeria, Somalia, Uganda, Eritrea, Bosnia, and Kosovo.

The religious use of violence *will* be with us in the new millennium, and it will behoove us to study its distinctively religious features. This is a lesson the U.S. Justice and Treasury Departments learned the hard way in the 1993 standoff in Waco, Texas. Federal agents surrounded the religious compound of a Christian apocalyptic group called the Branch Davidians, in an attempt to arrest its leaders. In the end, over eighty people met a fiery death. To prevent the repetition of such a tragedy, these government agencies have since consulted with scholars of religion from Harvard, Emory, and New York University on the nature of religious reasoning and group dynamics.[16] Small beginnings.

> None of the suicide bombers . . . conformed to the typical profile of the suicidal personality. . . . They all seemed to be entirely normal members of their families. . . . All were deeply religious.
>
> —*Nasra Hassan, Pakistani journalist*[17]

chapter 2

What Is Religion?

At the start of a semester I ask my students to define religion. They give me two sorts of responses, which I write on the board in two columns. In the first column go things like:

> Religion is belief in God.
> Religion is devotion to gods and divine beings.
> Religion is a time-honored tradition of norms and ethics.

or:

> Religion supplies comfort in times of crisis.
> Religion is an important ingredient in people's mental health.

As I explain to my students, these definitions are too limiting. They risk misunderstanding one religion in terms of another and exclude some religions altogether. Not all religions, for example, practice the worship of higher beings, and among those that do, not all see this activity as the defining feature of religion. In certain forms of Hinduism and most forms of Buddhism, the worship of gods is even regarded as an inferior path, suitable for the spiritually weak. Further, worship, belief, and devotion cover only a small portion of what one finds

> Just at the moment when it seems urgent to develop a more sophisticated understanding of religions, there appears to be little consensus about precisely what religion is and how it can best be studied.
>
> —*Mark C. Taylor*[1]

in religion. Love, ecstasy, fear, wonder, surrender, humility, and guilt also come to mind, as well as the activities of fasting, meditation, penance, mystical journeys, evangelism, pilgrimage, sexual abstinence, almsgiving, sacrifice, ordination rites, and theological speculation.

In the second column I put definitions like this:

Religion is an emotional crutch for the weak.

Religion arises from dreams and fear of ghosts.

Religion is a pre-scientific explanation of the natural world or a mistaken understanding of historical events.

Religion is created by societies to enforce their norms and values.

Religion is (as Karl Marx stated) the "opiate of the people," used to subjugate the masses.

To these I usually add:

Religion is the creation of visitors from other planets whose superior technology awed ancient peoples.

Religion stems from the human bicameral brain "speaking" to itself (à la Julian Jaynes).

Religion is obsessive behavior caused by psychological disorders (à la Sigmund Freud).

Religion has its origins in an inevitable mental error—a "disease of language" (à la Max Müller) or "virus of the brain" (à la Richard Dawkins).

The problem with these approaches is that they reduce religion to something else in order to understand it. Religion becomes "just" or "really" something else in disguise. Sometimes "reductionism," as this is known, is helpful. To assume that an irrational fear is really the internalization of a childhood trauma might be very therapeutic. In other situations, however, reductionism does not do justice to a subject. Few would agree that true love is "simply" a matter of hormonal imbalance or "really" the sublimation of the fear of loneliness.

> A lot of talk about religion often turns out to be about something else.
>
> —*Jeppe Jensen*[2]

That we should see religion as a subject in its own right—a "phenomenon"—and not something else in disguise is not a matter I can prove to a reader who has just begun the study of religion. Instead I must ask the reader to accept this judgment provisionally, just as a professor of art history might entreat a class of introductory students not to jump to the conclusion that impressionism is "just" the creation of nearsighted artists or that cubism is "really" the result of experimentation with mind-bending drugs.

What is needed, then, is a definition of religion that avoids the pitfalls of these two lists:

- It must not exclude any religion or aspect of religion.
- It must not promote the particular emphasis of one religious tradition over that of another.
- It must not compel us, prematurely at least, to reduce religion to something else.

A definition that meets these criteria runs as follows:

Religion is orientation to ultimate reality.

What this definition presumes is that every religion promotes a vision of a reality infinitely more important than anything else. Often referred to as "sacred reality," or "the sacred," or "the holy," this reality is contrasted with the "profane" world in which human beings live out their day-to-day existences. Precisely because ultimate reality is infinitely more important than anything else, all religions advance the conviction that human life reaches its *fullest* potential and becomes *most* meaningful when it is properly oriented to this reality. Hence religious people will risk privation, torture, and even death for their religion, which is why using force against a religious movement so often backfires. Given the choice between a secure life that lacks ultimate meaning and a life of hardships that is nonetheless justified by an infinitely meaningful reality, religious people, *to the extent they are religious*, will always choose the latter.

My qualifying phrase, "to the extent they are religious," is an important one because it isolates what is specifically religious in someone's behavior. Not everything religious people do is oriented to ultimate reality, even in an explicitly religious context such as a mosque or church. People take part in religions for many reasons that have nothing to do with orientation to ultimate reality—social, political, economic, moral, aesthetic, and cultural reasons. But to

Orientation to Ultimate Reality. Finding the canine vision of ultimate reality inadequate, this dog opts for conversion to something else. (From a *Pickles* cartoon by Brian Crane, Courtesy the Washington Post Writers Group)

the extent that orientation to ultimate reality is their purpose, we may speak of their activities as distinctively "religious."

By this measure we can also determine the boundaries between religion and kindred activities such as philosophy and ethics, romantic love, or even sports and hobbies. While all of these may be pursued with a "religious" dedication or passion, they only become truly religious when their final point of reference is something *ultimate*. So, too, we may draw a distinction between religion, on the one hand, and magic and spirituality, on the other. Spirituality is orientation to a higher, *but not necessarily ultimate*, reality (for example, a world of ancestral spirits); magic is manipulation of a higher reality that is *never* ultimate. Indeed, manipulation of ultimate reality is, by definition, impossible unless one becomes part of that reality; and then one has crossed over from magic into mysticism, a form of religion.

> The pubescent boy gazing soulfully into the eyes of the pubescent girl in a William Steig cartoon and murmuring, "There is something about you, Ethel, which gives me a sort of religious feeling," is, like most adolescents, confused.
>
> —*Clifford Geertz*[3]

In defining religion as "orientation to ultimate reality" we must also keep in mind that religion may not be the central interest in a person's life. This is not as paradoxical as it might at first seem, for it is possible to assign ultimate value to something and yet give little thought to it in the normal course of day-to-day life. In times of war people may sacrifice their fortunes or their lives for their country, but such patriotism may not be center stage in their peacetime, civilian existence. In religion, too, ultimate reality is not something that people focus on all the time. Unless we are speaking of the exceptional mystic or holy man, orientation to ultimate reality takes place by degrees and is restricted to certain times and places, even among "very religious" people.

Children and the newly initiated usually do not even have the capacity for such singular orientation; and many people are satisfied with very limited degrees of orientation to ultimate reality, such as Christians who attend church only on Christmas and Easter or are present only for their baptism, marriage, and funeral. Furthermore, as long as humans live in profane reality—which is the working premise of all religions—ultimate reality can never fully encompass their lives. There is no purely religious person, no simple *homo religiosus*. Instead, there is a broad spectrum, from the person who turns to prayer only as a last resort, to those who devote their entire day to religious activities. Thus, rather than ask whether this or that person is "religious," or whether Marxism or Confucianism or atheism is a religion, we should ask *to what extent* a person or ideology is oriented to ultimate reality.

From these considerations we must also conclude that not everyone who participates in a religion will be the best example of a religious person. It is not that these people are not religious, but as William James once suggested, we need to give our attention to the "virtuosos" of religion, not the amateurs or bystanders, if we want to discover religion's essential nature. Not everyone attending a performance of Mozart's *Magic Flute*, after all, is our best guide to uncovering the essential nature of opera.

The "task" or "business" of religion, then, is the activity of orientation to ultimate reality. And this task is made difficult by two factors. The first is the realization that human beings live in profane reality, which, by comparison to ultimate reality, is less real. Profane reality may be "evil" or illusory, or merely incomplete, but it is always the reality within which humans must work. The problem here is that all our thoughts, actions, and intentions have reference, in the first instance, only to this profane reality, making orientation to ultimate reality seemingly impossible. It is as though religious people are attempting to move into a fourth dimension, having at their disposal only three-dimensional tools and ideas.

A second problem is that most religions posit a buffer zone between the profane and the sacred. The two realities are not juxtaposed or separated by a void, but divided by other, *higher-order realities*. These are "higher-order" because, like ultimate reality, they are more real than the reality of the profane, human condition. They are not "ultimate," however, because they are inferior to ultimate reality and never the final object of orientation. Nor are these intermediate entities all "sacred," for they can encompass evil as well as good. The sorts of things that one finds in these buffer zones include angels and demons, ancestral spirits, and demigods; heavens, hells, and altered states of consciousness; and forces such as *karma*, *mana*, magical power, and sin. Whether friend or foe or indifferent force, these, as well as the disadvantages of living in the profane world, need to be negotiated to gain access to ultimate reality. They must be controlled, placated, befriended, or avoided—but how?

Religious people reach beyond the confines of profane reality and engage these higher-order realities through *symbols*. To understand how this works, we must first distinguish between two uses of the word symbol. In everyday parlance a symbol is something that "represents," "stands for," or "signifies" something else: The American flag *stands* for liberty, *signifies* patriotism, and *represents* the country's values. In a second sense, however, symbols are the means by which people *orient* themselves to the symbol's referent. Thus Americans sometimes get a shiver up their spines at a flag-raising ceremony. They feel connected in a metaphysical or spiritual way to a reality "behind" the

> Symbols . . . are like bridges. They enable us to link, to relate, to cross between one experience and another.
>
> —*Robert Ellwood*[4]

flag. This is also true of symbols in art, literature, and popular culture, which is why they have the power to inspire strong emotions and acts of heroism. If this were not so—if symbols in literature only "stood for" their referents—then every work of literature would tend toward allegory.

So it is symbols, in this second sense, that enable people to reach beyond the mundane world and interact with higher-order realities and ultimate reality. A statue of the Buddha is a powerful religious symbol, not because it depicts or "represents" the ideals of Buddhism (which it does), but because it orients Buddhists away from the illusory world that controls their lives and toward *nirvana*. Likewise, when a radio evangelist asks his listeners for their prayers and financial support, he is using the symbols of prayer and charity to orient both himself and his audience to God. Just how symbols are able to achieve this, and how religions select them in the first place, will be our focus in the next chapter.

chapter 3

RELIGIOUS SYMBOLS

Religious symbols can be *anything*. They can be buildings, works of art, discrete movements, entire rituals, plants, animals, persons, places, stories, con-
cepts, words, and sounds. A given tradition may designate a temple as the place
to meet God, shamans as the proper mediators between humans and spirits, acts
of mercy as an appropriate means of imitating the divinity, and a priest's bene-
diction as the correct way to receive blessings from heaven. There is nothing
that cannot be used as a symbol in some religion. *The only criterion for something becoming a symbol is that it be deemed by a religious tradition as an appropriate tool for orientation to ultimate reality.*

What makes a symbol "appropriate," in turn, is that it fits into the larger
system of meaning advocated by a religion. If a particular tradition envisions
ultimate reality as something that is "up there" in heaven, then the activity of
ascent might become an appropriate way of orienting oneself to it. Thus Moses
is reported to have ascended Mount Sinai to receive God's commandments, and
the ancient Mayans and Sumerians went to the considerable trouble of building
artificial mountains—pyramidlike temples and ziggurats—to approach their
gods. Ascending might not be appropriate, however, if one's intention is to honor
a river sprite or the god of the underworld. If one's profane existence is thought
to be controlled by malevolent powers, magical practices might be included in
one's arsenal of symbols. When Buddhism came to Tibet it embraced indigenous magical practices as a means of protecting its adherents from demons and
bloodthirsty goddesses, and in Christianity exorcism is still used to expel evil
spirits.

So symbols function by participating in the rationale or "logic" of a particular religious system, what we shall call its "inner-logic." This is why the
symbols of one religion are usually ineffective or meaningless in the context of
another, and why, to an outsider, a religion's repertoire of symbols can appear
chaotic or arbitrary. In Judaism, for instance, circumcision is the means by which
a male is brought into the covenant, joining the ranks of God's chosen people.
Yet for most Christians, circumcision, if practiced at all, is not a religious act,
but a medical procedure undertaken for hygienic or cosmetic reasons. In Zen
Buddhism an invitation to tea can be the occasion for meditation, enabling the

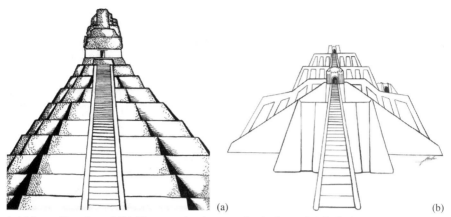

(a) Mayan Temple and (b) Ziggurat. Ancient peoples built artificial elevations so they could come into the presence of sky gods. Priests offered prayer and sacrifice in the upper chambers of these structures. Some biblical scholars think that the ill-fated Tower of Babel was a ziggurat. (Illustrations by Joseph Hamilton)

host and his guest to gain a glimpse of the Buddha-nature; but outside of Zen, tea is generally no more than an opportunity to socialize, with no theological implications.

If religion is orientation to ultimate reality, and this orientation requires the use of particular symbols that coincide with a religion's inner-logic, then it would seem that we have a theoretical basis by which to analyze religions. That is, we can gain considerable insight into a religion by identifying its symbols and its vision of ultimate reality, and then piecing together its inner-logic by observing how adherents use their symbols to orient themselves.

Suppose, for example, we approach the analysis of a religion by first identifying as many of its symbols as possible. That is, we attempt to establish the range of "tools" by which the members of a tradition orient themselves to ultimate reality. In some instances this task is fairly straightforward, for almost all religions use actions or objects that stand out from the ordinary. A Buddhist walking around an oddly shaped building, always in a counterclockwise direction; a Jain teacher traveling naked ("sky-clad") from town to town; or a Jewish man in the heat of a summer day wearing a hat and a dark suit, with a wool shawl under the suit jacket—these are all good candidates for religious symbols, for none of them seems aimed at the realities of this world, but at those of another.

In other cases it is not the unusual but the everyday that is enlisted by a religion as symbols; these are harder to spot. In Hinduism the occupation of grocer is a means of orientation, and among the Amish one is brought closer to God by living a simple, agrarian life. Showing respect for parents, telling the truth, and helping one's neighbor also qualify as symbols in many religions. In

Clothing as Symbol. An Orthodox Jew prays before the Western Wall in Jerusalem. His hat, dark suit, and prayer shawl (the tassels of which are visible just below his jacket) are ways in which he orients himself properly to God. (Courtesy www.HolyLandPhotos.org)

Unusual Objects. Sometimes religious symbols are things that have no purpose in everyday life. (Among archaeologists it is even standard practice to label strange finds "religious" objects.) This prayer wheel, used by Buddhists in the Vajrayana tradition, enables one to direct the prayer inscribed on the wheel into the universe by spinning the weighted ball around the handle. (Illustration by Joseph Hamilton)

still other cases, symbols are a matter of what people avoid or do *not* do, making it even more challenging to catalog the components of a symbolic system. It is not easy to observe someone *not* eating pork or roasted grain, *not* swearing or pronouncing the name of God, or *not* walking through a cemetery.

Once one has identified a substantial number of symbols, the second stage of analysis begins. This involves puzzling out the rationale by which the adherents of a religion deem these things (and not other things) the appropriate tools for orientation to ultimate reality. If one determined that a religion uses food offerings, then one could postulate that this religion envisions its god or gods as hungry beings. Cleansing rituals often indicate that adherents envision ultimate reality to be "pure" in some manner that profane reality is not. To move closer to ultimate reality, some sort of cleansing or purification is logically called for.

Instead of working from the perspective of a religion's symbols, one can also begin an analysis by determining a religion's understanding of profane and ultimate reality. While ultimate reality, by definition, can never be fully described, all religions provide enough information about ultimate reality for adherents to orient themselves to it in some initial fashion. If, as in our previous example, we can determine that a certain religion envisions God and his angels as "up there," then we may be able to understand many of that religion's sym-

Finding Ultimate Reality. All religions have a means of pointing adherents beyond this reality to ultimate reality. In this Chan Buddhist painting from the end of the seventeenth century, the artist uses the rocks, the lotus, and the ducks to frame his true subject: The sacred emptiness (sunyata) *that lies one step beyond the simplicity of the natural world.* (Freer Gallery of Art, Smithsonian Institution, Washington, DC: bequest from the collection of Wang Fangyu and Sum Wai, donated in their memory by Mr. Shao F. Wang, F1998.45)

bols as tools for human ascent or for encouraging the deity and his entourage to descend into profane reality. In devotional Hinduism it is helpful to begin with the knowledge that the god Shiva is envisioned as both ascetic *and* erotic. Otherwise the logic of combining sexual images with ascetic practices might escape us, leading us to the false conclusion that Shaiva practices are illogical and contradictory.

Thus, an analysis of religion can proceed from an inspection of its symbols or from its understanding of profane and ultimate reality. Because these approaches are not mutually exclusive, going back and forth between them often yields the best results. It is the same method we might use if we took a walk in the neighborhood and came upon a new construction site. To understand what the workers were trying to achieve and how they intended to achieve it—that is, the "inner-logic" of their activities—we might begin by attempting to determine the focus of their efforts. If this were a broken-down brick wall, we could work backward, so to speak, and develop an understanding of what tools might be appropriate: trowels, levels, and plumb lines. Or we could begin by inspecting the tools on site and develop a theory as to what the workers expected to accomplish with these trowels, levels, and plumb lines. To be safe, however, we would want to check our theories by going back and forth between the wall and the tools, watching the workers as they proceeded. We might be surprised. Perhaps the goal of the workers was not to repair the wall but to level it and use it as the foundation of a house they are building. Or we might discover that some of the tools at the site simply belonged to the workers' tool chests and had no bearing on the project at hand, which was to lay down loose bricks for a rustic patio in front of the crumbling wall.

To move us from construction sites to religions, and from theory to practice, part two will provide several examples of this sort of analysis of religions.

❧ Part Two ❧

Thirty Examples

The chapters in this part are hands-on, practical exercises. In the previous two chapters we have spoken of religion, ultimate and profane reality, and symbols in mostly abstract terms. Here we will focus on the actual practices of six religious traditions:

- Hinduism
- Buddhism
- Judaism
- Christianity
- Islam
- Primal religions

In each case I will identify the inner-logic of a tradition and explore several ways in which its adherents orient themselves to ultimate reality through symbols. My goal is to demonstrate how one can analyze religions using the definitions and the method described in the previous chapters. In choosing the examples for this part I have been guided by four objectives: to work with contemporary examples from each religion, to examine a variety of symbols, to avoid the bizarre and the sensational, and to limit myself to five symbols or groups of symbols within each tradition. Because of these objectives, the following examples are not intended as comprehensive treatments of these six traditions.

◄chapter 4►

HINDUISM

We begin our hands-on analysis of religions with Hinduism, a religion practiced by some 811 million people, mostly in India. This religion has no founder. It began in the sixth century BC and is a synthesis of traditions that extend back into the second and third millennia BC.

THE CASTE SYSTEM

Hindus envision ultimate reality as approachable in an almost unlimited number of ways. As their theologians express the matter, there are 330 million deities to whom one may turn. Consequently, Hinduism is unusually rich in symbols and possibilities for orientation. One of these is the caste system. In traditional Hindu thought there are four classes of people:

- Priests or "Brahmins"
- Nobles
- Commoners
- Serfs

These are ranked relative to one another, depending on their perceived proximity to ultimate reality. The Brahmins, who are considered especially close to ultimate reality, are on the top of society, followed by the nobles, the commoners, and the serfs.

The four classes are, in addition, divided into subgroupings called "castes," of which there are thousands. These are hereditary rankings that further define one's proximity to ultimate reality within one's class. For example, some Brahmins, by virtue of the family into which they were born, are closer to ultimate reality than other Brahmins. Finally, below the four classes is a large group of people (somewhere between 100 and 200 million) who are outside the rankings of the class system. They are known as "untouchables" and are considered the most distant of all from ultimate reality.

Thus, at birth one is given an identity that specifies his or her relationship to ultimate reality. One is either close to it or far from it, meaning that one's

330 Million Gods. The façade of this Hindu temple in Lanham, Maryland, reflects the many possibilities for orientation to ultimate reality available to Hindus. (Will Deming)

existence is more or less meaningful—more or less real—in comparison with others in Hindu society. Depending on class and caste, as well as age and gender, an individual is assigned a set of duties that must be performed in order to maintain his or her status relative to others and relative to ultimate reality. These duties, called *dharma*, specify one's occupation, proper conduct toward other members of society, and proper interaction with higher-order realities such as ancestors, sages, and gods.

Dharma is also the means by which Hindus can negotiate a higher-order reality known as *karma*, which can aid or obstruct one's orientation to ultimate reality. *Karma* is the force, either good or bad, that results from one's actions. Good *karma* comes from proper observance of one's *dharma*, bad *karma* from violating *dharma*. This force accumulates during one's lifetime and eventually discharges itself on its creator. Among other consequences, it produces rebirth in a new life, determined by the quality of one's *karma*.

Bad *karma* can bring about rebirth into a lower caste or class. If it is particularly bad it can result in rebirth in nonhuman forms—a snake, an insect, a bird—or into one of the many Hindu hells. Here one remains, sometimes for millions of years, until the effects of bad *karma* are exhausted through punishment. If, on the other hand, one accumulates sufficient amounts of good *karma*, he or she is reborn into a higher caste or class, or into a Hindu heaven, where a person can commune with the gods.

With these basic facts about the caste system in hand we could proceed as many before us have done. We could explore its origins and development in the ancient world: why there were originally three classes and how the fourth came into being through the integration of Indus Valley and Indo-European peoples, or how the upper three classes once shared a ceremony known as the investiture with the sacred thread, undertaken today only by Brahmins. We could investigate how the caste system has fared in the modern world: how foreigners, once considered demonic, have been assimilated into Hindu society; how untouchables have become the "scheduled classes," thereby gaining some degree of entry into the Indian educational system; or how the caste system has been eroded by the Western-style economies of large cities such as Delhi, Mumbai (Bombay), and Calcutta. We could also explore the number and diversity of the occupations divided among the castes, as well as what, to outsiders, appear to be anomalies—for example, even though Brahmins and most everyone else in India wear leather sandals, touching and working with leather is considered so defiling that it is suitable only for untouchables. Finally, we could subject the social inequalities of the caste system to Marxist, feminist, or postmodern critiques.

While any of these might be of interest, and all of value, focusing on these matters obscures the *specifically religious* character of the caste system. From the often overlooked perspective of a religious analysis, it becomes clear that the duties, occupations, and lifestyles of these various social groupings are so many religious symbols, and that in the minds of most Hindus, the caste system serves primarily to map out a vast symbolic system by which they can orient themselves to ultimate reality. Through the *dharma* of his or her caste, which Westerners often describe as unjust and oppressive, a Hindu can connect with a world that is more stable, more real, and more desirable than anything offered by Western society. In everyday life, every movement and thought has the potential of transcending and giving ultimate meaning to one's existence.

Now that we have identified the symbolic value of the caste system, it remains to explore what we have called its "inner-logic." That is, given that the duties of the caste system are understood to be effective tools for orientation to ultimate reality, *why* are they understood in this way? And why are *they* seen as appropriate, and not other actions such as undertaking a pilgrimage to Mecca or praying before a crucifix? What is it about the Hindu vision of ultimate reality that points to *dharma* as a reasonable way to bring oneself into harmony with it?

> Religion legitimates social institutions by bestowing upon them an ultimately valid ontological status, that is, by *locating* them within a sacred and cosmic frame of reference.
>
> —*Peter Berger*[1]

In exploring a symbolism as vast as the caste system we must necessarily speak in approximations and generalities. Even so, it seems fair to say the following. While Hinduism approves of a variety of ways to approach ultimate re-

The Caste System

Rigveda 10.90

The Man has a thousand heads, a thousand eyes, a thousand feet. He pervades the earth everywhere and extends beyond for ten fingers' breadth. The Man himself is all this, whatever has been and whatever is to be. . . . When the gods spread the sacrifice, using the Man as the offering, spring was the clarified butter, summer the fuel, autumn the oblation. They anointed the Man, the sacrifice, born at the beginning, upon the sacred grass. . . . When they divided the Man, into how many parts did they disperse him? What became of his mouth, what of his arms, what were his two thighs and his two feet called? His mouth was the Brahmin, his arms were made into the nobles, his two thighs were the populace, and from his feet the servants were born.[2]

This early mythical account from Hinduism's most authoritative scripture, the *Rigveda*, explains how the gods created and ordered our world: They sacrificed a primal, cosmic Man. When he is dismembered, human society comes into being, divided into four classes: Brahmin, noble, commoner, and serf. The message here is that society's class structure originates in ultimate reality. Members of Hindu society who wish to orient themselves to this reality must perform the duties (*dharma*) of the class into which they were born.

ality, ultimate reality itself, sometimes called *brahman*, is seen as a single whole. It is a unity that is vast and encompassing. It is the basis for the cosmos, whose diversity is but an expression of ultimate reality's richness and depth. Hells and demons; mountains, rivers, and forests; animals and human beings; ancient sages and the gods are all emanations from this single point, and like light refracted in various ways off the facets of a singularly beautiful gem, they form the marvelous illusion, or *maya*, that is our world.

Human beings fit into this unified world order as an ordered society, the classes themselves having emanated from *brahman* at the time of creation. For human beings to move from the periphery to the center, from the illusion to the source, they must first take stock of their respective places in the whole, which are their castes. They can then begin the process of further orienting themselves to ultimate reality by performing the *dharma* of their castes.

Because traditional Hindu society is divinely ordained, it is morally wrong to circumvent its hierarchy. A higher-order reality, the law of *karma*, regulates conduct. Those who resist the correct order of the cosmos are moved further away from its center and basis. Their lives become more illusory and inconsequential. Those who harmonize their lives with the structures of ultimate reality move toward it. Their lives take on greater reality, becoming more whole and more important.

This, then, is what I am calling the analysis of religion. The symbols of a religion are not random. They work within a larger system according to a "logic" dictated by a religion's vision of ultimate reality. By identifying a religion's symbols and delineating this logic, we may discern how a religion "works," as well as why it has appeal. Without such an analysis, we would not fully understand one of the most powerful sources of motivation in Hindu society. We would also be at a loss to explain why the caste system, now officially censured in India, is dying such a long, slow death—if it is really dying at all. Indeed, a system that offers so much meaning to so many people in so many different ways is more likely to transform itself than die.

DEVOTION TO A SUPREME GOD

While most Hindus participate in the caste system as a means of orientation to ultimate reality, they also make use of the many other symbolic systems within Hinduism. One such system is *bhakti*, or devotional Hinduism, which is closer to what Westerners understand as religion. This is the practice of devoting oneself to a supreme god. The two most popular supreme gods in Hinduism are Vishnu and Shiva, who are understood by their followers to be *brahman*, or ultimate reality, itself. Since these gods are ultimate, they exist beyond the reach of *karma*, and they have the ability to save human beings from *karma*'s effects. Hindus devote themselves to these gods, therefore, for the purpose of circumventing *karma* and the other higher-order realities that would otherwise determine their existence. In this way, they end the process of rebirth into profane reality and are joined forever to ultimate reality. The forms of devotion deemed appropriate—that is, the symbols of this particular variation of Hinduism—find their inner-logic in the way in which followers of these gods envision Vishnu and Shiva, respectively.

The Indian faiths comprehended under the term Hinduism have an almost unlimited diversity.

—*David S. Noss*[3]

Of the two gods, Vishnu is the most popular, claiming almost 550 million devotees. His followers envision him as a god who lovingly sustains the universe for the well-being of humanity, appearing at certain critical points in history to rescue or enlighten those who devote themselves to him. When Vishnu ventures into our reality, he must adopt a form that allows him to cross over from ultimate reality into profane reality without compromising the infinite nature of his being. These forms are called *avatars*. In all, Vishnu has ten *avatars*. One is the legendary king Rama, the hero of India's great epic poem the *Ramayana*. Crossing over into profane reality at a time when his devotees were threatened by outsiders, Rama chases the invading forces back to the island country of Sri Lanka. Devotees of Vishnu who are drawn to this *avatar* celebrate his heroic deeds in art, poetry, theater, and song.

Another *avatar*, familiar to many Westerners, is Krishna. The most famous moment in the life of this *avatar* is recounted in the *Bhagavadgita*, a document that Krishna's devotees distribute as scripture in public places, such as airports, much like Christian evangelists might distribute copies of the New Testament. In the *Bhagavadgita*, which means "Song of the Lord," Vishnu appears to the great king Arjuna at a decisive point in the latter's struggle against the evil usurpers of his throne. Vishnu, as Lord Krishna, or "*Hare* Krishna," advises Arjuna of his religious duties, and in so doing reveals to him the superiority of orienting himself to ultimate reality through devotion to Vishnu. Vishnu, Arjuna discovers, is the source and sustainer of the cosmos, the ultimate reality through whom and for whom all things exist. By devoting oneself first to Vishnu, one performs one's *dharma* in the best possible way, thereby taking the most direct path to what is real and true and meaningful in life.

Orienting oneself to Vishnu by honoring Krishna as Lord is one possibility. But one may also worship the baby Krishna, just as Christians sometimes give adoration to the baby Jesus as a means of orientation to their god. Krishna as mischievous toddler and teenage cowherd are also possibilities for envisioning and relating to ultimate reality through this *avatar*. Devotion to the teenager Krishna is popular among young people. Boys relate to him as loyal, trusting companions; girls approach the god as adoring lovers.

Shiva, in contrast to Vishnu, is understood as the master of powerful cosmic forces, especially as they bring about creation, destruction, and the endless cycle of birth, death, and rebirth. His followers, who number just over 200 million, often envision Shiva as expressing his mastery over these forces through withholding or flaunting his sexual potency. Here the process of human procreation has been employed as a cipher for understanding and relating to the activities of a god.

Creation is a product of Shiva's consummate eroticism. When he is sexually active, the cosmos comes into being and its life forms thrive. When he renounces sexuality, however, he assumes an austere, ascetic mode, and death and destruction enter the cosmos. Thus, the unrelenting and brutal interchange of life and death and well-being and pain that controls our reality is not only the will of this great god, but also a mere by-product of the magnificent reality in which he chooses to live. Indeed, his followers envision profane reality—our reality—as nothing more than the sound waves that emanate from a small drum Shiva plays when he dances. Those who orient themselves to Shiva through devotion to his erotic or ascetic powers do so out of love, as well as out of respect and fear. In return, they receive the grace to depart this insubstantial, karmic

Krishna Steals the Butter. In orienting themselves to the god Vishnu, many Vaishnavas approach him through the avatar *Krishna. Here, as mischievous child, Krishna is caught "stealing" butter, an offering sacred to the god, and therefore his to take. Krishna's naughty antics as a child reveal his ultimate reality to his devotees. Those who devote themselves to the child Krishna adore him like a mother would adore her own child.*
(Will Deming)

existence and be united with him in his reality forever. One form this devotion can take is the practice of sexual asceticism. In this way, devotees honor Shiva by imitating him. Just as Shiva withdraws himself from the life-giving aspects of our world, his followers abstain from their part in human procreation, thereby orienting themselves to his divine ways to the degree they are able in this life.

PUJA

Devotion to Vishnu, Shiva, and the many other gods of Hinduism can also take the form of *puja*, or service to the god through stylized social interaction with a statue, or "idol." Using a statue as a symbol, devotees express their love, respect, and gratitude for a god by engaging the god in acts of hospitality. For instance, one might shower a statue with milk, yogurt, and honey to nourish the god, or one might place fruit or coconuts before the image. Dressing the image and applying makeup, fragrances, and garlands are also proper ways of interacting with a god. Following these actions, the god will reciprocate, through the priest, by giving holy water and fruits or nuts to the worshipers.

Continual attendance on the god may be offered by lighting an oil lamp called a *kerala*. This is a tall lamp that serves as a stand-in for human worshipers. The base of the lamp is the person's feet, its column is the trunk of the body, and the oil dish on top is the head. When lit, the lamp's flame is understood as divine wisdom coming to the person from the god. As long as the lamp

The Kerala *Lamp. A Brahmin (Hindu priest) poses with a ker-ala lamp, a symbol used to offer extended periods of service* (puja) *to a god. While the oil lamp burns in the presence of a statue, the god associated with that statue imparts divine wisdom to his or her devotees. The string that the Brahmin is wearing across his chest and abdomen is the "sacred thread" of* kusha *grass, which gives him his status as a priest. The markings on his forehead are made with ashes and sandal-wood paste that derive from of-ferings. They orient him to the god Ayyappa, the son of Shiva through Vishnu, who appeared to Shiva in female form.* (Will Deming)

stands by a statue, devotion is being offered to the god, and as long as the lamp burns, grace is being imparted from the god to the worshipers.

The statues used in *puja* can be images of the god or images of higher-order realities that are dear to a particular god. For example, one can offer de-votion to an image of Vishnu himself; to an image of Laksmi, Vishnu's female counterpart; or to Garuda, the divine bird on whom he travels. Likewise, one can honor Shiva by showing hospitality to his sexual consort Parvati, his bull Nandin, or one of his two sons: Skanda, who has six heads and multiple arms, and Ganesha, the elephant-headed god. Ganesha is especially popular, since he is the patron god of good beginnings and removing obstacles from one's life. Before getting married, going off to college, or starting the day, a Hindu might orient him or herself to ultimate reality by making an offering to Ganesha.

Another important image used by the devotees of Shiva is the *lingam*, or phallus. Like the other statues, the *lingam* is showered with milk and honey, and adorned with robes, perfume, and flowers. While the adoration of Shiva's erect penis may seem to Westerners completely incongruous with "genuine re-

(a)   (b)

Orientation to Vishnu. The devotees of Vishnu (Vaishnavas) can worship him in a variety of ways—directly as Lord Vishnu, through one of his earthly appearances (avatars), *or through one of his entourage. Shown here are (a) Vishnu's wife Lakshmi, whose four arms indicate her many powers, and (b) Garuda, Vishnu's mount or "vehicle." Usually portrayed as a female bird, Garuda appears here as a winged devotee wearing Vishnu's mark on his forehead. He has been adorned with clothes and a fresh garland.* (Will Deming)

(a)   (b)

Orientation to Shiva. The god Shiva can be worshiped as Lord Shiva or he can be approached through his consort, one of his sons, his "vehicle," or in the form of the lingam. *Shown here are (a) Shiva's mount or "vehicle," Nandin the bull, kneeling in front of a* lingam; *and (b) Shiva's elephant-headed son, Ganesha, holding an orange he has been offered. The three horizontal lines on his forehead are Shiva's mark.* (Will Deming)

Shiva's Lingam *Pictured as the Creative, Powerful, World Pillar. Arising out of the primeval chaos, Shiva creates the cosmos through his* lingam. *The gods Brahma (as a swan) and Vishnu (as the boar* avatar) *appear in very light relief on the upper and lower left of the statue, vainly searching for the beginning and end of Shiva's infinite powers. Worshipers have performed acts of* puja, *clothing the statue, leaving flowers, and applying cosmetics. One worshiper has left a coin (lower right).* (Will Deming)

ligious devotion," Shiva's followers do not see the *lingam* as indecent or pornographic. Rather, it is one means to orient themselves to Shiva's awesome powers of creation and destruction. Here Westerners are reminded, in a rather dramatic way, that religious symbols can be *anything*, as long as they accord with the inner-logic of a religion.

OM *(AUM)*

The most important scripture of Hinduism is a collection of chants known as the *Rigveda*, or "verses of wisdom and praise." These chants have been memorized and passed down by priests, generation after generation, and are believed to have emanated from *brahman* itself at the beginning of time: They are cosmic reverberations of ultimate reality that we can experience in our reality. One who hears them comes into contact with ultimate reality through the medium of sound; one who speaks them *participates*, in some small measure, in this reality.

Om *(AUM). Of the sounds (or* mantras*) used as symbols in Hinduism,* Om *is the most encompassing. Pronounced in the proper way, it orients one to the undifferentiated essence of* brahman.

Since the chants of the *Rigveda* have such an intimate connection with ultimate reality, Hindus regard even the syllables of the words they contain as powerful symbols. The most powerful among these, in turn, is the syllable *Om,* whose written form in Sanskrit, the ancient language of Hinduism, is familiar to many Westerners.

When pronounced or heard, this syllable provides one access, variously, to the fullness of the *Rigveda,* the underlying essence of existence, or the god of the cosmos, whose wisdom and being are otherwise inscrutable. In some Hindu traditions its pronunciation is seen as a tool that brings one closer to the ultimate by stages. Understood as a contraction of the letters A-U-M, *Om* moves one, via the sound waves of our reality, past the reality of everyday, conscious existence (A), to the reality of our imaginations and dream worlds (U), to the undifferentiated reality that we experience in dreamless sleep (M). Finally, the resonance, and then the silence, that follows the "M" carries one, ever-so-briefly, to the edge of ultimate reality. Here a sound, "aum . . . ," has become a powerful symbol.

THE DIVINE KNOWLEDGE (*JÑANA*) AND YOGA

A final symbolic system in Hinduism, practiced by an influential minority of Hindus, is the path of "divine knowledge" (*jñana*). The adherents of this variation of Hinduism hold that ultimate reality is actually more accessible if we turn away from the world outside us—the world of *dharma,* reward and punishment, the gods—and focus our energies inward. Because *brahman* is the source of everything in the universe—the final essence and truth of all things, including human beings—it is, they believe, equivalent to a "world soul." Since human beings also find the roots of their existence in a soul (*atman*), they conclude that *brahman* is, in fact, identical with *atman.*

The notion that *brahman* (or god) dwells within each person is actually a commonplace among Hindus today. The distinctiveness of the path of divine knowledge is its emphasis on disciplines of self-mastery and self-actualization.

Atman Is Brahman

Chandogya Upanishad 6.8.6–7

When a person in this world dies, my dear one, his speech enters his mind, his mind enters breath, breath enters heat, and heat enters *brahman*. The entire world has as its soul that which is the most subtle of all things: that is Truth; that is *atman*; that is *you*, dear Shvetaketu.

In this dialogue, from one of the early scriptures of the Hindu way of divine knowledge (*jñana*), a father reveals to his son the identity of *brahman* with *atman*.

The *dharma* of one's caste ceases to function as a primary symbol, and *karma*, heaven and hell, and the gods also become less relevant. In their place, one seeks access to the divine knowledge that, down deep, one *is brahman*.

Since this is knowledge that pertains to what is infinitely real and true, it has the power to transform a person completely. It is not, in other words, a knowledge that one acquires in the normal (profane) sense, as one might "learn mathematics." The difference between this knowledge and the knowledge of our profane existence is as great as the difference between reading about a near-death experience—for example, a plane crash—and surviving one. The latter transforms a person in a way the former cannot.

Divine knowledge, then, is a knowledge that must be experienced and encountered. This takes place through symbols such as controlled breathing, dietary restrictions, physical postures, and meditation—practices collectively know as "yoga." While most Westerners know of yoga only as a means of promoting health and relaxation, in Hinduism it is a tool that enables the practitioner to gain control over every aspect of his or her life forces ("yoga" is related to the English word "yoke"). Only when this is achieved can a person orient his or her life forces inward, toward *brahman*. Otherwise, these forces disperse themselves outward, through the senses, into the profane world, becoming confused in their relation to *brahman*.

Whereas those who practice the *dharma* of their caste seek to orient themselves to *brahman* by interacting harmoniously with this exterior world, those who follow the path of divine knowledge "interiorize" religion. Their goal is to circumvent the symbolic systems of social duty, karmic retribution, and rebirth and be absorbed directly into *brahman* once and for all.

⊰chapter 5⊱

BUDDHISM

Buddhism began in India shortly after Hinduism appeared. It was founded by a former Hindu, Siddhartha Gautama (ca. 563–483 BC), who is known to Buddhists as Shakyamuni, "the sage of the Shaky clan," or Buddha, "the enlightened one." Today Buddhism is hardly practiced in India. Most of its 359 million adherents live in Sri Lanka and the east Asian countries of China, North and South Korea, North and South Vietnam, and Japan. Certain forms of Buddhism, especially Zen, are also popular in the United States.

NIRVANA AND THE FOUR NOBLE TRUTHS

Buddhism shares many of Hinduism's presuppositions about profane and higher-order realities. Among these are a belief in the karmic system of retribution and the endless cycle of birth and rebirth, called *samsara*. Yet Buddhism does not share Hinduism's vision of ultimate reality. Instead of *brahman*, Buddhists orient themselves to the final "blowing out" of this life, or *nirvana*. This is because Buddhism rejects the Hindu notion of an eternal soul. Like the illusional world of the profane reality in which we live, Buddhists hold that "we," too, are fleeting and insubstantial. We are like a flame, which has no permanent core, or like a "piece" of the wind. The profane world only *appears* to be purposeful, stable, and substantive; but everything and everybody is in existential flux. For this reason, too, profane "reality" is filled with suffering, since the fleeting "I" desires equally fleeting "things," and consequently "I" can never be satisfied, never reach closure, never accomplish "my" goals.

Because Buddhists also regard most theological speculation as part of the illusory, profane world, elaborate discussions about the nature of ultimate reality are deemed *in*appropriate as tools for orientation. For this reason, Buddhism, perhaps more than any other religious tradition, is reticent to discuss the details of its vision of ultimate reality. As we just saw, their preferred term for ultimate reality is a negative one: *nirvana*, the "blowing out" of this existence. It orients one to ultimate reality by indicating what it is not: It is not *samsara*.

Rather than speculate on the nature of ultimate reality, Buddhists pursue a "practical" approach to religion embodied in the Four Noble Truths. These

"All Is Suffering"

One concept that is particularly hard for non-Buddhists to grasp is the Buddhist notion of suffering (*dukkha*). When Buddhists claim, in the first Noble Truth, that "all is suffering," they do not mean that there is nothing pleasant or enjoyable in profane and higher-order realities. Rather, they are insisting that any pleasure or satisfaction one encounters here comes at a terrible price: endless attachment to an unreal, meaningless world. This necessarily leads to suffering, either in this life, or in the next, or in the next. Thus, finding joy in this existence is likened to one who licks honey off the edge of a razor blade. At first there is enjoyment, but this will be followed by pain and regret.

Truths describe profane reality and encourage adherents along a disciplined "path"—a regime of symbolic acts—that leads to release from it. Here are the Four Noble Truths in their traditional form, side-by-side with a version of it in our language of analysis:

1. All is suffering.

   (1) All profane and all higher-order realities are disorientation from ultimate reality.

2. All suffering is caused by craving.

   (2) All disorientation is caused by the attempt to attach oneself to things that are not real.

3. All suffering can be ended.

   (3) It is, in fact, possible to end all disorientation.

4. The way to end all suffering is to follow the Noble Eightfold Path.

   (4) The way to end all disorientation from ultimate reality is to dedicate oneself to symbolic practices known as the Sacred Eightfold Way.

The "Noble Eightfold Path" mentioned in the fourth Noble Truth is a program of orientation away from things closely identified with profane reality. It encompasses such things as "right views" (such as acceptance of the Four Noble Truths), "right aspirations," "right speech," and the "right means of livelihood." More concretely, Buddhists practice several forms of renunciation as symbols. Chastity is demanded for laypersons, and celibacy for certain orders of monks and nuns. Buddhists also renounce deceit; occupations that destroy life; entertainments such as dancing, singing, and drama; alcohol and other intoxicants; and luxuries such as jewelry, perfume, and soft bedding. In the inner-logic of Buddhism, these acts of renunciation are seen as the appropriate tools for orienting "oneself" to *nirvana* because, as practices of self-denial, they reduce "one's" participation in the (non-real) world of profane "reality."

THE THREE JEWELS OF REFUGE

While Buddhists are intentionally obscure about the details of *nirvana*, their understanding of profane and higher-order realities is quite explicit. These realities are inhabited by the gods, as well as five other classes of beings (see later in this chapter). In Buddhist thought, all of these beings suffer, and all are in need of *nirvana*. Thus, in contrast to Hinduism and most other religions, Buddhism does not locate the gods in ultimate reality. As a result, acts such as reverence for the gods and prayer operate very differently as symbols in Buddhism. While the gods may be more powerful than humans, and capable of both bestowing blessings and raining down evil, they are not able to give anyone access to ultimate reality.

In Buddhism, then, the gods play only a secondary role. Along with other superhuman beings—demigods, hungry ghosts, and hell beings—they are feared, worshiped, honored, and placated, but they never take center stage in the religion. Instead, the path to *nirvana* is accomplished largely through self-effort. While the gods and other higher-order realities may be able to grant one health and long life as aids toward this end, they can do little more. In fact, Buddhists believe that humans have this one advantage over even the gods: Humans can attain *nirvana* while the gods cannot.

An important set of symbols in Buddhism, therefore, includes things that support a person in his or her own self-effort. These are the Three Jewels of Refuge: the Buddha, his teachings (*dharma/dhamma*), and the Buddhist monastic community (*sangha*). The Buddha, for instance, serves as a role model and source of inspiration. Because he has attained the highest, or final, *nirvana*, he is completely beyond any interaction or connection with our reality. Even so, his historical existence in our world inspires us. It bears witness to the fact that the Four Noble Truths are true; that the Noble Eightfold Path does indeed lead to *nirvana*; and that *nirvana* can be attained by any informed, determined human being. Consequently, in one's attempt to escape *samsara*, one "takes refuge" in the actions of the historical Buddha. Similarly, one takes refuge in the other two jewels of Buddhism: One studies the Buddha's recorded teachings and takes guidance from those who have already made considerable progress along the Noble Eightfold Path, namely, Buddhist monks and nuns.

To understand better the role of self-effort in Buddhism, let us consider the following metaphor. Suppose someone wanted to become an accomplished weightlifter. Prayer might help, but prayer alone does not give one big muscles.

Likewise, one needs a healthy body, good nutrition, and the financial means to pursue weight training, and for this reason weightlifters are more or less mindful of doctors, dietitians, and sponsors. Yet, even with these advantages in place, it is still necessary to put forth a great deal of self-effort, for no one has the ability simply to "give" someone a powerful physique.

To meet the challenge of this self-effort, weightlifters usually find it necessary to "take refuge" in several things that function much like Buddhism's Three Jewels. They hang posters of Arnold Schwarzenegger and other greats on their walls for inspiration. They study the techniques and advice of these masters. And they join a gym, where they train with the encouragement and camaraderie of those headed down the same path.

In like manner, because Buddhism envisions the gods as excluded from ultimate reality, it accords more importance to self-effort than do most other religions. "Taking refuge" in the life, the teachings, and the accomplished followers of the Buddha consequently function in this religion as fundamental symbolic actions.

As a concrete example of how one might "take refuge in the Buddha," we may cite the use of *stupas*. A *stupa* is a structure that contains a relic from the Buddha's life. This can be a tooth, a piece of bone, or a splinter from his begging bowl. It can also be a picture or an object of particular value that relates to the historical Buddha. When *stupas* are large structures or buildings, as they often are in Asian countries, they are decorated with scenes from the Buddha's

Taking Refuge in the Buddha Through Stupas. *This stone relief from a South Asian* stupa *built around* AD *200 depicts the Buddha in the moments just before his enlightenment. Tempted by the demon Mara and his minions to give up his quest for* nirvana, *the Buddha nonetheless prevails. By meditating on such heroic scenes from the Buddha's life, Buddhists gain direction and encouragement on their own path to enlightenment.* (Freer Gallery of Art, Smithsonian Institution, Washington, DC, purchase F1949.9)

(a)

Miniature Stupas. *In the United States one sees mostly miniature* stupas. *Shown here are* stupas *in the (a) Cambodian and (b) Japanese traditions. The brass altar* stupa *from Sri Lanka (c) stands in front of the standard offerings of flowers and a candle.* (Will Deming)

(b)

(c)

life, allowing pilgrims to reflect on his many trials and accomplishments. In Buddhist temples, on the other hand, one usually finds miniature *stupas*, which offer non-pilgrims an opportunity to take refuge in the Buddha. By visiting *stupas* of either type, adherents find the necessary encouragement to appropriate for their own lives the Buddha's singular achievement, the extinguishing of *samsara*.

Statues and paintings of the Buddha are yet other symbols that provide refuge. Usually depicting the Buddha in deep contemplation in a seated position, these images present him as the role model par excellence for those seeking ultimate reality through meditation. Out of reverence for his dedication, his success, and his willingness to share the path to *nirvana* with all humanity, Buddhists leave flowers and fruit and burn incense and candles before the image. These are not gifts to the Buddha, however, for he is not a god nor is he any longer in contact with our reality. Rather, they are offerings made as solemn acts of commitment to the challenge he sets before them.

Still other images of the Buddha depict him on his deathbed. According to tradition, the Buddha's life ended anticlimactically: He died of food poisoning. Rather than see this as an embarrassment, however, Buddhists take refuge in his death as a confirmation of the first Noble Truth—that our present existence necessarily leads to suffering and sorrow. Through these images of a *reclining* Buddha, adherents experience the final moments of the life that the Bud-

Statue of the Buddha. All Buddhist altars have a statue of the Buddha from which one can gain a sense of what it means to achieve ultimate reality. This statue is in the Theravada tradition. The offerings before it include fresh flowers, fruit, candles, and incense (in the brass bowl behind the fruit on the right). The top of a stupa *can be seen behind the candle on the far right corner of the table.* (Will Deming)

(a)

(b)

The Reclining Buddha. Buddhists often take refuge in the reclining Buddha. Here they experience the calmness of the Enlightened One, even at the moment of his death, when he was in great pain. (a) The small brass reclining Buddha is from Sri Lanka; (b) the monumental reclining Buddha belongs to a Cambodian temple. (Will Deming)

dha extinguished, thereby finding direction for extinguishing their own lives. If the artist has done his or her job, they will see in the Buddha's facial expression, especially in his eyes, a symbol that makes the achievement of *nirvana* palpable.

DEFERENCE TO THE SIX BEINGS

Even though the worship of a god or gods cannot, in itself, orient one to ultimate reality in Buddhism, Buddhists attend to the gods as well as to five other classes of beings in the profane and higher-order realities. While none of these beings can eliminate life's suffering, proper orientation to them can at least further one's quest for *nirvana*. Consequently, Buddhists accord these beings various degrees of honor, devotion, and deference through symbolic acts. The six classes are animals, human beings, demigods, gods, hungry ghosts, and hell beings.

Since none of these beings has attained *nirvana*, and all suffer from the unrelenting illusion of birth, death, and rebirth, Buddhists deem it proper to show them compassion. Engaging in acts of compassion toward all beings orients a person to ultimate reality in two ways. First, it produces positive *karma*, which mitigates one's suffering in this and future lives; and second, it diminishes the illusion that one is an individual with a self or ego separate from others. Both outcomes bring one nearer to *nirvana*.

For example, most Buddhists are strict vegetarians. They do not eat any animals, the class that includes all sentient life forms on earth other than human beings. They also show compassion toward animals to the extent that they will not kill rodents or garden pests. Beyond this, Buddhists interact with each class of beings according to the influence that it might have on their lives. Hungry ghosts, for instance, can disrupt one's efforts toward *nirvana*, and thus need to be fed. This can be done at home or by Buddhist priests in a temple. The standard offerings are rice and water, sometimes in a stylized meal of seven grains of rice and a few teaspoons of water. Oatmeal is also used. Many Buddhist communities placate these ghosts annually by opening up the temple to them for a day, enticing them in with candy, soft drinks, and other treats.

Demigods such as "*dharma* protectors" and "*dharma* kings" have the power to supply health and wisdom and to fight ignorance in one's life. These beings are worshiped with prayers and offerings, much like gods in other religions. Malevolent beings, on the other hand, which include various gods, demigods, and hell beings, must be kept at bay. Sometimes this is done by placating them, sometimes by gaining control over them through practices of meditation and magic.

Hungry Ghosts. Two Mahayana priests stand near an altar for hungry ghosts at the entrance to their temple. At certain times of the day, rice and water will be placed here, both out of compassion for these ghosts and in the hope that they will stay out of the temple. (Will Deming)

In forms of Buddhism influenced by the Tibetan tradition, for example, profane reality is understood as an illusion controlled by powerful demons, gods, and goddesses. It is these malevolent higher-order powers, not simply the impersonal force of *karma*, that keep human beings in bondage to *samsara*. To attain *nirvana*, one needs to overcome them, a task for which Tibetan Buddhists employ several magical techniques.

In one ritual, a Tibetan monk constructs miniature houses to trap a particular demon or divinity. He lures his victim in with a combination of meditation and items like rice and red string, symbols believed to attract unsuspecting higher-order powers. In other rituals, monks seek to become higher-order beings themselves by stealing the power of their superhuman foes. First, a monk will "create" one of these foes in his mind through meditation. He visualizes it in minute detail, down to the color and weave of its clothing and its choice of jewelry. This may take many months or even years of disciplined meditation. Once this vision has become as real for the monk as the equally illusional and unreal world of his profane reality, he works to disarm his creation and acquire its power. For this purpose he employs additional symbolic tools called *mantras* (powerful sounds) and *mandalas* (powerful diagrams). His goal, finally, is to acquire all the power of his created reality and to take his position in it as

(a)   (b)

Mandalas. *This Tibetan* mandala *(a), created with colored sand in the 1990s, helps a person situate himself or herself with respect to the various powers and realms of the cosmos. The unreal, sensory world of our existence is indicated by the objects in the corners and the scenes of suffering and death around the perimeter (see detail, b). As one moves inward, passing through bands of flames, lightening bolts (*vajras*), and lotus petals, one crosses into the realms of higher-order powers. At the center of the* mandala *is a divine palace, guarded at its four gates by terrifying monsters. Inside are chambers for nine gods. The blue thunderbolt of Yamantaka, the Conqueror of Death, stands in the center chamber.* (Minneapolis Institute of Arts: Gift of the Gyuto Tantric University; 3M; Construction Materials, Inc.; and the Asian Art Council) supreme ruler. Having created his own profane reality and its governing higher-order realities, and having taken control of it, he rises above its constraints and attains *nirvana*.

BODHISATTVAS AND BUDDHAS

Between the six classes of beings and the *nirvana* that the Buddha has attained, many Buddhists recognize another group of beings known as *bodhisattvas*, "beings of enlightenment." These are Buddhists who are on their way to becoming buddhas themselves, but have not yet entered the "final," or "highest," *nirvana* of the Buddha. Instead, they voluntarily defer their entry into final *nirvana*, pledging to save other beings from *samsara*. From either a heavenly state of enlightenment, called the *samboga-kaya* (not to be confused with the heavens of the gods), or an earthly mode of appearance, called the *nirmana-kaya*, they interact with human beings, encouraging them, teaching them, and granting them boons. In return, the proper human response—the appropriate symbolic action—is to honor these enlightened beings with offerings of flowers and incense and pray for their blessings. The most popular *bodhisattva* is known under the Indian name Avalokitesvara, "the one who looks down from heaven."

Bodhisattvas. *The Indian* bodhisattva *Avalokitesvara ("the one who looks down from heaven") is known to Chinese Buddhists as the female* bodhisattva *of compassion, Kuan Yin, patron of childbirth and family. Here she pours out compassion onto her devotees from a small vase in her right hand.* (Will Deming)

Eventually *bodhisattvas* gain the status of buddhas as they advance toward final *nirvana*. With this new status they create heavenly paradises, devoid of the limitations and suffering of our profane world. As a gift to humanity, they allow devotees to be reborn into these "pure lands," where *nirvana* is more easily attained. The Buddha of the Western Paradise, known in China as Amitabha and in Japan as Amida, gives his followers access to his pure land if they pronounce his name in the salutation, "Hail Amitabha (or Amida) Buddha." By persistently and earnestly pronouncing this formula, devotees are able to hear the voice of Amitabha calling them out from the profane world. Here a short salutation has become the principal symbol of a religious tradition.

MEDITATION (ZEN)

Chan Buddhism, which originated in China around the sixth century AD, is better known to most Westerners in its Japanese form and pronunciation, "Zen." Rather than envisioning ultimate reality in the original Indian sense of "blowing out," practitioners of Zen orient themselves to what they call the "Buddhanature." Drawing on the ancient Chinese concept of the Universal Way, or *Tao* (pronounced "dao"), Zen's inner-logic contends that one gains insight into ultimate reality by removing the countless misconceptions he or she uses to interpret life. Accordingly, the favored symbolic tool in Zen Buddhism is medi-

Active Meditation. In planting and tending herbs, this Zen monk practices meditation by engaging in routine movements. Mindful only of his work, his thoughts rest in the present, disengaged from any past experiences or future plans. (Will Deming)

Seated Meditation. As a model for Buddhists who practice seated meditation (zazen), *this statue depicts the Buddha sitting calmly astride a beast, who represents craving and emotional tumult.* (Will Deming)

tation, which is what *zen* (*chan*) means. Just as seeing into the depths of a pond is best accomplished by letting the ripples on the surface settle, rather than diving in and creating more disturbance, meditation is the appropriate tool to establish a line of vision to ultimate reality, which is currently obstructed by the disturbances of the profane world.

Sometimes this meditation is performed in the midst of repetitive tasks such as gardening, flower arrangement, pottery, doing laundry, or mopping a floor. Zen Buddhists have found that the routine of these activities is an excellent tool for disengaging one's mind from its profane business of analyzing, calculating, planning, and achieving. As the body moves in expected ways, one's thoughts rest effortlessly in a timeless present, a state called "mindfulness."

In Zen one can also meditate by simply sitting still. The usual seated position resembles a pyramid, which brings the weight of one's body into equilibrium so that it will not distract the mind. This position is sometimes also thought to allow certain "winds" (*prana*) to circulate freely in the body. In some schools of Zen, practitioners combine seated meditation with still other symbols, known as *koans*. These are enigmatic statements or questions designed to push one out of normal, profane thought processes. The most famous *koan*, perhaps, is: "You have heard the sound of two hands clapping. What is the sound of one hand clapping?" Others include:

A man sees a friend in a window. Is the friend inside or out?
A dog is running through the forest. Is she chasing or being chased?
A woman washes dishes. Is her husband at home?

Meditating on a *koan* orients one to ultimate reality by overloading the mind's logical, profane capacity to solve problems. When this happens, one's normal interaction with the world is interrupted. One "knows differently" and attains a glimpse of ultimate reality.

chapter 6

JUDAISM

Judaism began in the second millennium BC as the religion of the ancient Israelites. During most of the first millennium BC its symbolic system relied heavily on a central temple in its capital city, Jerusalem. Modern-day Judaism has its roots in the first century AD, after the destruction of the temple. There are currently more than 14 million Jews in the world, most of whom live in the United States and Israel.

MONOTHEISM AND IDOLATRY

Jews envision ultimate reality as a supreme god whose worship excludes the worship of any other god or being. This understanding, called monotheism, has resulted in many symbols that involve *avoiding* certain things that are associated with the worship of other gods. The most prominent of these is Judaism's prohibition of idolatry, or the use of images in worship. This excludes both images of other gods, naturally, and images of God himself. Thus, in sharp contrast to Hinduism and Buddhism, Jewish places of worship have no statues. Here, because performing a particular action *dis*orients one from ultimate reality, *avoiding* that action has become an important symbol.

THE NAME OF GOD (YHWH)

All religions prohibit things that disorient their adherents from ultimate reality, so the rejection of images is by no means unique in the way it functions as a symbol in Judaism. Likewise, all religions prohibit the use of certain things that are "too sacred" or "too holy." This is the claim that these symbols are too closely connected to ultimate reality to be used, except perhaps in situations where the distance between profane reality and ultimate reality can be bridged. A good example of this in Judaism is the holy name of God. Jews refer to God using a variety of titles and descriptions: the Most High, the Holy One of Israel, the God of Abraham. And because Judaism has only one god, Jews often simply use the generic designation "God" to refer to ultimate reality. But the

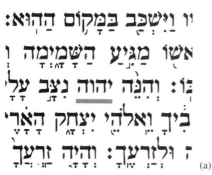

The Call of Abram

12 Now the LORD said to Abram, "Go from your country and your kindred and your father's house to the land that I will show you. 2I will make of you a great nation, and I will bless you, and make your name great, so that you will be a blessing. 3I will bless those who bless you, and the one who curses you I will curse; and in you all the families of the earth shall be blessed."

4 So Abram went, as the LORD had told him; and Lot went with him. Abram was seventy-five years old when he departed from Haran. 5Abram took his wife Sarai and his brother's son Lot, and all the possessions that they had gathered, and the persons whom they had acquired in Haran; and they set forth to go to the land of Canaan. (b)

(a)

The Name of God. Because the proper name of God is not pronounced in Judaism, it is often printed without vowels, as in (a) (underlined, third line). All ancient Hebrew was originally written without vowels, and the Hebrew alphabet to this day has only consonants and two semi-vowels (y and w/o). On those occasions when vowels need to be indicated, a system of "pointing" with dots and lines is used. Here, while the words around the divine name have been pointed, the name itself has been left as four consonants. In English translations, the divine name is rendered "LORD," with small caps, as in the story of Abraham's call (b). By contrast, "Lord," without small caps, translates the Hebrew word Adonai. (Will Deming)

Jewish god does have a personal name, like Vishnu and Ganesha, yet most Jews will not pronounce it.

The personal name of God first appears in the Torah, the basic document of Judaism (see later in this chapter). In ancient Hebrew, which is written without vowels, it appears only as four consonants: YHWH. Modern scholars of Judaism usually hold that these four consonants were vocalized as "Yahweh" and made reference to the ultimate reality of God: "I am," "I exist," "I have the power of existence and being." In the ancient Near East, however, as in many cultures, names were used as symbols for gaining special access to the holder of the name, and even for gaining power over him or her. As a result, pronouncing the name of God eventually became the prerogative only of a high priest—that is, it became a privilege of the person in Judaism considered closest to ultimate reality.

With the destruction of the centralized temple in the first century AD, the office of high priest vanished. Since that time, the personal name of God has not been used in Jewish worship. Furthermore, when the language changed and classical Hebrew fell into disuse, vowels were added to the Torah to facilitate its study and public reading. The name of God, however, was never vocalized. Today it is either left without vowels, replaced by *ha-Shem* ("the Name"), or given the vowels of a word that was pronounced in its place. In this last instance, when readers come to the name YHWH in a text, they say *Adonai*, a word that means "my Lord." Alternatively, if one mixes these two words, pronouncing the consonants of YHWH with the vowels of *Adonai*, one arrives at some version of "Jehovah," which is the origin of that name. In English translations of the Torah, YHWH is sometimes translated "Jehovah," and sometimes translated "LORD" with small caps, to distinguish it from "Lord," which translates *Adonai*. In handwritten copies of the Torah in Hebrew, one is never allowed to erase the name. If, in creating the scroll, a scribe makes a mistake in writing it, the leather on which it is written must be cut from the scroll and the hole repaired with a patch.

THE COVENANTS, THE TORAHS, AND THE COMMANDMENTS

The principal way most modern Jews define their relation to ultimate reality is in terms of agreements, or "covenants," between them and God. While God is understood to be the Creator of the universe and hence the god of all peoples, he nonetheless has a special relationship with the Jews by virtue of their ancestral ties to Judaism's founder, Abraham. According to Jewish tradition, God spoke with Abraham, initiating a covenant with him and his descendants. Later God spoke with Moses, one of these descendants, adding an additional covenant. Moses, in turn, is said to have recorded part of this covenant in writing and to have passed down the other part orally. These are known as the Written and the Oral Torahs, *torah* being a Hebrew word for "instruction" or "guidance."

Together, these Torahs determine most of Judaism's symbolic system. The Written Torah, sometimes simply referred to as *the* Torah (as in our discussion above), is fundamental for the Jewish understanding of ultimate reality. Consisting of the first five books of the Bible (Genesis, Exodus, Leviticus, Numbers, and Deuteronomy), it recounts God's creation of the world, his disappointment with early human beings, his covenants with Abraham and Moses, and his interaction with the first Israelites. One of the most important of these interactions is known as the Exodus. During the Exodus, God is said to have rescued the Jews from slavery in Egypt and established them as a nation in their own right on the eastern shores of the Mediterranean Sea.

The Written Torah also contains 613 *mitzvot*, or "commandments." These provide Jews with direction for proper orientation in all aspects of life. Among them are prescriptions for the way Jews should dress, prepare meals, marry, and conduct business transactions, and for how Jews should treat fellow Jews and those of other religions. The well-known practices of circumcision, Sabbath observance, and keeping kosher all derive from these commandments. Likewise, the Oral Torah also contains instructions, but in even greater detail.

Because the Torahs are so fundamental for defining Judaism's symbolic system, reading, studying, and meditating on them are deemed to be important symbolic acts as well. In synagogues—Jewish places of worship—the liturgy

The *Shema*

Deuteronomy 6:4–9

Hear, O Israel: The Lord is our God, the Lord alone. You shall love the Lord your God with all your heart, and with all your soul, and with all your might. Keep these words that I am commanding you today in your heart. Recite them to your children and talk about them when you are at home and when you are away, when you lie down and when you rise. Bind them as a sign on your hand, fix them as an emblem on your forehead, and write them on the doorposts of your house and on your gates.

This is the beginning of a passage from the Torah know as the *Shema* (the first word of the passage, "Hear!"). The *Shema* begins by proclaiming God's exclusive, monotheistic relation to the Jews, and then prescribes ways in which adherents can learn the Torah's commandments and pass them on to future generations. The demand that they be bound "as a sign on your hand" and fixed "as an emblem on your forehead" is the basis for the use of phylacteries—leather boxes containing sections of the Torah (see page 91). Jews "write them on the doorposts" by affixing small cases containing scripture to door frames, both at the entrance to a building and on inside doors. These cases, known as *mezuzahs,* contain the entire *Shema,* written on parchment by a scribe. The *mezuzah* in the photo has a hinged door and latch so the parchment inside can be checked periodically to see if it is still intact. The Hebrew word on the front of this *mezuzah* is *shalom,* "peace, well-being."

The Oral Torah. This is a page from the Talmud, an imposing collection of rabbinic scholarship. The center text is a portion of the Oral Torah; the texts around it provide interpretation and practical application from hundreds of learned rabbis and their disciples.
(Will Deming)

requires that the Written Torah be read out loud, in its entirety, at least once a year. Jews gather weekly or several times a week to hear these readings, and it is common for Jewish children to learn ancient Hebrew so they can read and hear the Written Torah in the original language. Many Jews also wear prayer shawls (*tallit*) and phylacteries (*tefillin*). The former have fringes tied in special knots at the corners, as specified in the Torah. During synagogue services and in private prayer, Jews wrap themselves with these shawls as a way of bringing all the commandments of the Torah to mind. Phylacteries, in turn, are black leather boxes that contain short passages from the Written Torah. In preparation for weekday services, Jews affix them to their foreheads and hands with leather straps so as to keep the commandments "constantly before them."

Since the sixth century AD, the Oral Torah has been available in a document called the Talmud. This document, which contains some two and a half million words, combines commandments from the Oral Torah with an expansive commentary on their meaning. The religious leaders of Judaism, called rabbis ("masters," "teachers"), acquire authority in their communities based on their proficiency in the Talmud. Some are even held in awe for their comprehensive and exacting knowledge of this document.

TORAH SCROLLS

Just as the study of the Written Torah has become an important symbol in Judaism, the physical scroll used for reading it to the congregation also serves as

Torah Scrolls. The Written Torah, in scroll form, is the primary symbol of Jewish communal worship. By hearing it read in the synagogue, Jews become familiar with the will of God and the agreements that exist between themselves and God. A pointer (yad) lies on the middle column of the scroll. To the right, one can see a seam where the sheets of leather have been sewn together. (Will Deming)

a powerful means of orientation to God. Every synagogue is required to have a traditional Torah scroll—a handwritten copy of the Written Torah in Hebrew on a scroll of vellum or parchment. These scrolls are prepared at great expense from ritually clean ("kosher") materials, according to exacting religious standards. It is not uncommon for a scroll to cost $15,000–$20,000.

When not in use, a Torah scroll is kept in a special case called an ark. Here it is covered with an embroidered cloth made of velvet or silk and adorned with

Scroll Ornaments. Because of their importance as symbols, Torah scrolls are treated with great deference. These two scrolls have been wrapped in traditional velvet covers, the cover on the right proclaiming them to be the "crown of instruction" (keter torah). The left scroll wears a silver "breastplate." On the right scroll hangs a silver yad (reading pointer), and its staves are topped with silver finials (also called "pomegranates"). (Will Deming)

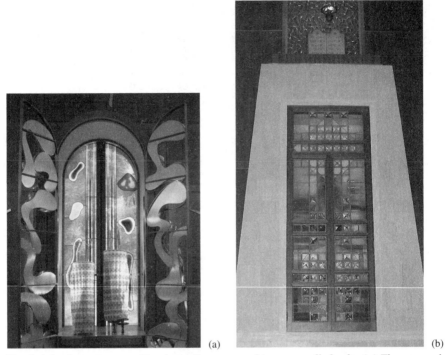

(a)

(b)

Torah Arks. In synagogues, Torah scrolls are stored in cases called arks. (a) The open ark contains two Torah scrolls. Its contemporary design features brass gates instead of the traditional doors and a stained glass window as its back wall. (b) Above the closed ark one sees the eternal flame, identifying the Torah as God's divine light. (Will Deming)

a crown or two finials and a decorative "breastplate," all made of silver. Above the ark is always an "eternal flame," identifying the Torah as God's wisdom. When a Torah scroll is removed from the ark for public reading, it is held open for the congregation to witness and placed on a podium called the *bimah*, where it becomes the focal point of the sanctuary. During the reading, the reader may use a silver pointer (*yad*) to follow the words, so as not to touch the text with his or her finger. If a scroll becomes worn out to the point that it cannot be satisfactorily repaired, it must be stored permanently in a safe place or given a formal burial. It is sinful (disorienting) to throw it away.

THE WESTERN WALL

As noted earlier, ancient Jews used a central temple as the primary means to orient themselves to God. This temple was important because it marked the location of ultimate reality in the profane world. It was God's "house," where one

The Western Wall. A Jewish man touches the Western Wall in Jerusalem as he prays to God. To his right, one sees the prayers of others, written on small pieces of paper that have been rolled up and inserted into cracks between the stones. As the most prominent part of the temple plaza still standing after the temple's destruction in AD *70, the Western Wall orients visitors to the former residence of God in Israel.* (Courtesy www.HolyLandPhotos.org)

found special opportunities for orientation. Jews traveled from all parts of the ancient world to come into the presence of God, to pray, offer sacrifices, and attend religious festivals supervised by priests. Originally constructed in the tenth century BC, the temple was destroyed in the sixth century BC by the Babylonians. Shortly thereafter a second temple was built. This temple stood until the first century AD, when it was destroyed by the Romans, never to be rebuilt.

After the destruction of the second temple, Jews continued to visit the site for purposes of orientation. Since ultimate reality had once dwelt in profane reality on that spot, adherents believed that it could still be used as a meeting point between the two realities. Because most of the temple complex had been burned and leveled by the Romans, only a few structures remained visible above the rubble. One of these was a retaining wall that had supported the western side of the temple plaza. Because it was still standing, and because the western side of the plaza had been the closest to the temple, Jews began to use this "Western Wall" as a place of pilgrimage and prayer.

In Judaism today the Western Wall still functions as an important symbol. Jews orient themselves to God there by expressing grief over the loss of his house (hence its other name, the "Wailing Wall"), and it is an especially auspicious place to read the Torah and submit requests to God through prayers, sometimes written on slips of paper and inserted into cracks in the wall. Here is an example of an architectural ruin as symbol.

⊰chapter 7⊱

CHRISTIANITY

Christianity began in the first few decades of the first century AD as a type of Judaism. After the death of its founder, Jesus of Nazareth, his followers declared him to be a leader of the Jewish people chosen by God himself—the "messiah," or "Christ." They further maintained that God had raised Jesus from the dead and allotted him a place in ultimate reality. Today Christianity has 1.9 billion adherents, which is about a third of the world's population.

THE TRINITY AND GOD THE SON

Christianity, like Judaism, Islam, and a few other religions, envisions ultimate reality as a solitary, exclusive God. Christians, however, also understand God as three interrelated but distinct "persons," each of whom needs to be taken into account for the purposes of orientation. Ultimate reality, which is referred to as the "Godhead" or the "Trinity," includes God the Father, God the Son, and God the Holy Spirit. That ultimate reality is both divided in this way and at the same time still a single, "monotheistic" unity is an instance of the religious claim that ultimate reality surpasses the logic of profane experience.

Of the three persons of the Trinity, Christians designate God the Son as the necessary starting point for orientation to ultimate reality. In the Christian view, human beings, on their own, are incapable of orienting themselves to God in an acceptable manner. They are imperfect, "unrighteous" beings separated from a perfect, righteous god by their "sins." For this reason, God the Father had to *orient himself* to human beings through God the Son. He sent his son into profane reality as a human being, Jesus of Nazareth, to atone for the unrighteousness of humanity. Thus, Christians understand Jesus' life and death in the world to be the means by which God established the necessary conditions for orientation: Jesus, "the Christ," the one sent by God, has provided his followers, "Christians," a way to ultimate reality.

The principal symbols in Christianity, therefore, are things that orient adherents to ultimate reality through God the Son. These include belief and public testimony that Jesus is, in fact, God's divine son; acts of praise, adoration, and reverence for Jesus in various forms—Jesus as baby, as teacher, and as

God the Son. This ancient and still popular image of a fish indicates the importance Christians assign to God the Son in orienting themselves to ultimate reality. The letters in the image spell the Greek word "fish" (ICHTHUS), *an acronym for the claim that "Jesus is the Christ, the Son of God and Savior."* (Will Deming)

"Lord" in heaven; and conduct in everyday life that emulates Jesus' conduct while he was on earth.

By far the most important act in Jesus' life was the suffering he endured at his crucifixion. Charged with blasphemy and sedition, he was condemned to death by a Roman governor, nailed to a large wooden cross and left to die. Christians believe that Jesus' suffering on the cross was the definitive expression of God's love. God, in the form of Jesus, sacrificed himself freely and selflessly for humanity. As a result, many Christian symbols enable adherents to imitate Jesus by "participating" in his crucifixion, and Christians sometimes describe acts of orientation to God as "bearing the cross of Christ."

Charity to the poor, for example, is seen as a way Christians can "give sacrificially" to others. Similarly, in preparation for Easter, the Christian celebration of Jesus' resurrection from the dead, most Christians observe a forty-day period called Lent, during which they give up certain favorite foods and comforts and reflect on the suffering (often called the "passion") of Jesus. As part of this reflection, many Christians also visit the "stations of the cross." These are fourteen images, usually affixed to the walls of a Christian sanctuary, that depict moments from the final hours of Jesus' life, as he was escorted to the cross, crucified, and then buried. During this visit, Christians meditate on each incident and address Jesus in prayer.

BAPTISM

Baptism is the rite by which someone becomes a Christian. Upon the profession of faith in Jesus Christ as the Son of God, either by oneself or, if the person being baptized is a child, by a sponsor, the initiate is sprinkled with or immersed in water. On the one hand, baptism is understood as an act of "washing," cleansing away the sins that separate one from God. More in line with the distinctive inner-logic of Christianity, however, baptism is also interpreted as an act of "dying" to the profane world in imitation of Jesus' death. One is said to be "buried with Christ" in baptism. In this way, baptism becomes a symbol that ends a person's profane existence and initiates him or her into an existence oriented to ultimate reality. He or she is "born again" to a new life.

The Passion of Christ. Jesus' trial and crucifixion—his "passion"—hold a central place in the inner-logic of Christianity. Shown here are some of the many symbols that orient Christians to his suffering: (a) a crucifix (a cross with a dying Jesus); (b) an image of Jesus with a crown of thorns; and (c) a central "altar" on which the sacrifice of Jesus is reenacted during the eucharist. (Will Deming)

The context for this new life, in turn, is the church, understood as "the body of Christ." It is a realm of orientation to God formed from Christ's resurrected body. As a way of glorifying Jesus after his crucifixion, God is said to have released him from death and provided him with everlasting life and a body that is no longer a part of the profane world. This body now serves as a haven of refuge and salvation for Christians, who describe themselves as baptized "into the body of Christ," and consequently "parts" or "members" of this divine communion.

THE EUCHARIST

In contrast to baptism, the eucharist is a symbol for those who have already become Christians. Known also as the "Lord's Supper," it is a stylized meal con-

The Stations of the Cross. During Easter (as well as other times of the year), Christians re-flect on the fourteen stations of the cross. This is station twelve, just after Jesus dies. On the right, a Roman soldier confesses his faith in Jesus as the divine Son; below, a follower kneels in adoration; and on the left, Jesus' mother and the disciple John (with halos) mourn his death. (Will Deming)

Dying with Christ. By undergoing baptism, initiates to Christianity "die" to the profane world, are "buried with Christ," and then rise to a new life in Christ's divine body (the church). The "cruciform" shape of this particular baptistery provides a visual orientation to Jesus' suffering on the cross. (Courtesy Christ the Teacher Chapel, University of Portland)

The Real Presence. Christians who believe in the "real presence" of Christ in the eucharist place any consecrated bread that is left over from the eucharist in a chest called a tabernacle. Here it is reserved for the needs of the sick and the dying and serves as a focus of religious adoration. This ornate tabernacle belongs to St. Mary's Cathedral in Portland, Oregon. (Will Deming)

sisting of bread or wafers and wine or grape juice. These are used as tools for orienting Christians to God through Jesus' death by means of his body and blood, respectively. By eating these symbols, Christians incorporate the Son's suffering and compassion into their own bodies. The majority of Christians also believe in the "real presence" of Jesus in the bread and wine. After a priest's blessing, the bread and wine actually *become* his flesh and blood, with the result that God once again crosses over into profane reality in the body of Jesus. Understood in this way, the eucharist becomes an ongoing point of contact between profane and ultimate reality.

Just as baptism has a social dimension to it, establishing people as members of the "body of Christ," so also with the eucharist. By receiving and ingesting ultimate reality through the eucharist, the divine nature of Jesus' self-sacrifice becomes part of them, enabling them to imitate his sacrificial love. They are empowered to show the same love toward one another that God showed humanity through Jesus. For this reason the eucharist also goes by a third name: "communion," meaning fellowship, community, sharing. It is in communion, especially, that Christians become "brothers and sisters" of one another in the "family" of God the Father. If the occasion arises that Christians must choose between profane family ties and their religious siblings, it is often the expectation that they will choose the latter, for these are allegiances based in ultimate rather than profane reality.

THE VENERATION OF MARY, MOTHER OF GOD, AND THE SAINTS

All Christians believe in higher-order realities. These might be the regions of Heaven, Purgatory, and Hell, or beings such as angels, demons, and Christ's archenemy, Satan. Likewise, most Christians also believe in higher-order beings called "saints." These are Christians whose lives of exemplary orientation to God have earned them a special closeness to God in the afterlife. Christians

Mary and the Saints. Many Christians devote themselves to higher-order beings called saints. Mary, the mother of Jesus, is considered the foremost among the saints. (a) The statue depicts Mary with Saint Ann, her mother. (b) The image of Mary in the devotional alcove shows her holding the baby Jesus. The letters above her and beside Jesus are Greek abbreviations for "Mother of God," and "Jesus the Christ." (c) The classified ads offer thanks to Mary, Jude, and Claire for prayers answered. (Will Deming)

still living in the profane world pray to them, asking the saints to intercede for them before God.

Certain saints, moreover, are believed to be particularly effective in championing this or that cause or profession. These include "lost causes" (Saint Jude), "lost things" (Saint Anthony), the profession of nursing (Saint Catherine of Siena), and bee and animal husbandry (Saint Ambrose). Saints have been adopted as "patrons" of churches, towns, and organizations, in order to provide these entities with a special orientation to God; and individuals are oriented to God through their "Christian name"—the name of a saint they receive at baptism. By far the most important saint is the Blessed Virgin Mary, the mother of Jesus. For the many services she performed as the "Mother of God" (God the Son), she has become the patroness of numerous things, especially motherhood, faith, joy, obedience, suffering, and glory. Under the name Our Lady of Guadalupe, she is considered to be the patron Saint of the Americas, thereby orienting Christians in the Western Hemisphere to God.

Interaction with the saints usually takes the form of devotion to images and statues in the Roman Catholic tradition and to paintings known as "icons" in the Orthodox tradition. The latter are understood as "windows into heaven," or instances in which God becomes present in the profane world, echoing the incarnation of God in Jesus. For Mary, it is common to light devotional candles or "pray the rosary" before her, during which one reflects on the fifteen religious "mysteries" of her life. Devotees often use a string of counting beads (a "rosary") to keep track of their place in the ritual.

GUIDANCE AND AUTHORITY

Christianity has no comprehensive, universally accepted canon of instruction, like the Talmud, for orientation to ultimate reality. Instead, each Christian denomination has its own tradition of religious law, while Christianity as a whole has stressed the importance of interacting with the third person of the Trinity, the Holy Spirit, in order to discern God's will. Christianity holds that all adherents have received the "indwelling of the Spirit," which enables God, through the Holy Spirit, to guide each Christian individually. The Spirit manifests itself in people's lives variously, however, and consequently different denominations of Christians hold differing views on how God communicates most authoritatively with his adherents.

In the Roman Catholic church, which numbers just over one billion members, God is thought to communicate most authoritatively through leaders of the church called bishops, especially the bishop presiding in Rome. He is known as "His Holiness" or the "Pope," a title that identifies him as the spiritual "Father" of the church. His role includes issuing directives to the church inspired by the Holy Spirit, and convening councils of bishops, who, through the promptings of the Spirit, discuss and resolve issues facing the church.

(a)

(b)

Religious Authority. (a) Every Catholic church has an "ambry." This is a cabinet holding three containers of oil used in orienting Catholics to God—in baptism, in illnesses, and in the consecration of priests. For the oil to function as a symbol it must first be blessed by a bishop. In this way, each church receives its authority to orient its parishioners to ultimate reality through a bishop. A bishop's own church is called a cathedral, literally his "chair" or "seat" of power. (b) It contains an actual chair on which only bishops can sit. When the bishop of Rome, the Pope, issues his most authoritative directives to the church, he is said to speak ex cathedra, *"from his chair."* (Will Deming)

Among Orthodox Christians, who number some 215 million, the matter is similar. These Christians are oriented to God through several large, self-governing churches (Greek Orthodox, Russian Orthodox, etc.). While these churches recognize the legitimacy of each other's orientation, each has its own spiritual leader, called a patriarch ("paternal head" of the church), who is understood to have the final word in determining the will of the Spirit.

In Protestant forms of Christianity, by contrast, divine guidance is more often understood as coming in an authoritative form directly to the individual. These Christians number around 342 million. While they also have hierarchies that oversee their particular denominations (for example, Lutheran, Methodist, Baptist), they give much greater emphasis to the role of sacred scripture. Bible study, with the aid of the Spirit, is their principal source of divine guidance.

Finally, Christians who identify themselves as "Pentecostal" or "Charismatic"—be they Catholic, Orthodox, Protestant, or some other affiliation—believe that the Holy Spirit communicates directly with individuals on a regular basis, bypassing other forms of religious authority. On these occasions, they are "filled with the Holy Spirit," who enables them to prophesy, speak in unknown languages, and heal the sick through God's power. Thus, within Christianity, there are several possibilities for envisioning how ultimate reality exercises authority in the profane world.

⊰chapter 8⊱

Islam

Islam began in the seventh century AD with the appearance of Muhammad the Prophet in the area now known as Saudi Arabia. Spreading quickly beyond Arab territories, it now has about 1.2 billion adherents. These live mostly in the Eastern Hemisphere, in the geographical area defined by Senegal and Morocco to the east, Estonia and Kazakhstan to the north, Indonesia to the west, and Madagascar and Mozambique to the south—although relatively few Muslims live in Russia, Mongolia, China, or other east Asian countries, which are also in this region of the world. According to many experts, Islam is the world's fastest growing religion.

ISLAM AND *SHIRK*

Ultimate reality in Islam is envisioned as "Allah," which is simply Arabic for "God." Much like the god of Judaism and Christianity, Allah is singular and exclusive. He alone is the proper object of orientation, and Islam's inner-logic derives from the principle of complete submission to God's will in all areas of life. The word "Islam," in fact, means "surrender," and adherents of this religion call themselves "Muslims," or "ones who surrender" to God.

The refusal to orient oneself to God, on the other hand, points to one's involvement in *shirk*, a term that describes "associations" or "allegiances" in the profane world that prevent an unqualified surrender to God. In Islam, the proper worth and function of everything in the world is determined by God. To use or assign value to something from another perspective is to usurp God's authority.

For example, Islam teaches that wealth is a blessing from Allah. But if one uses wealth only to benefit oneself, one has become involved in *shirk*, for wealth is given by Allah to benefit both an individual and his or her family and community. One of the five *minimum* obligations of a Muslim, therefore, is to give a percentage of his or her net worth every year to the poor. Only in this way can a Muslim "purify" his or her wealth for other uses. Indeed, the word used in Arabic for "almsgiving," *zakat*, literally means "purification."

67

Almsgiving

Qur'an 107.1

Have you considered the man who denies the Last Judgment? He is the one who sends the orphan away and discourages others from feeding the poor.

Giving to the needy of one's community is one of the five most basic ways to orient oneself to God in Islam. In this passage from the Qur'an, Islam's most holy book, one who refuses to give alms is identified as a man who risks eternal disorientation from ultimate reality.

Another example relates to the Islamic concept of society (*umma*). All Muslims belong to God's society and are equally the servants of God. For one Muslim to give preference to another on account of race, socioeconomic status, culture, or national identity is *shirk*. It establishes unauthorized associations that disrupt the world community established by God. This particular doctrine is actualized every year in the Islamic pilgrimage to Mecca, the *Hajj*. During the *Hajj*, Muslims from all over the world come to Mecca, in Saudi Arabia. Here they worship God at Islam's central shrine, the Ka'bah, and perform other acts of piety in and around Mecca. The Saudi government, in turn, is required by Islamic tradition to open its borders to anyone who is Muslim, regardless of nationality or political stance. This is true even when Saudi Arabia is at war with its Muslim neighbors.

MUHAMMAD AND THE QUR'AN

Muhammad, who lived from about AD 570 to 632, is understood by Muslims to be "the Prophet of God." This means that one needs to orient himself or herself to Allah through Muhammad. Unlike Jesus in Christianity, however, Muhammad is not considered divine. Rather, he delivered God's message to humanity and lived a life in complete and perfect surrender to God. To please God, Muslims must internalize this message in their lives and imitate his deeds.

The message that Muhammad delivered is contained in a book called the Qur'an. Muslims hold that this book is not the creation of Muhammad, but an earthly copy of a heavenly original, dictated by God through the Prophet. It is a direct communication from God for the ordering of human life on earth, and so Muslims view the Qur'an as the proper basis for all religion, law, ethics, and human institutions. Thus in Muslim countries there is no uniquely secular law, for every just law derives in one way or another from a precedent in the Qur'an. Likewise, it is scholars and lawyers for the most part, not religious profession-

Religion and Society

The guidance provided by the Holy Qur'an prescribes appropriate rules and limits that govern the relationships between parents and children, men and women, employee and employer, and so forth, in every possible situation. . . . Islam has solutions that work for all problems that face society—immorality, destruction of family life, care of the young and old, AIDS, teenage pregnancies, crimes, and so on and so forth. Trying, as other religions attempt to do, to create a moral human being without creating a moral society is equivalent to teaching a man to ski and then putting him on a mountain without snow.[1]

This statement, from an Islamic brochure, is typical of the Muslim understanding of the role of religion in society. The religious teachings of the Qur'an, as interpreted by Islamic jurists, are the proper basis for all morality, all law, and all human endeavor.

(a)

(b)

The Shahada. *Islam's concept of ultimate reality and its symbolic inner-logic are summarized in the* shahada, *a declaration of faith that every Muslim makes:* La ilaha illa Allah, Muhammad rasul Allah: *"There is no god but God, and Muhammad is His messenger." In this way a Muslim declares that ultimate reality is an single, monotheistic God and that proper orientation is achieved by imitating Muhammad's life and adhering to his message. The* shahada *is sometimes (a) used in full, and sometimes (b) shortened to its first clause.* (Will Deming) als, who are the religion's leaders and authority figures. Known as *ulemas*, they function simultaneously as jurists and theologians. They pore over the Qur'an, ancient accounts of the Prophet's life (*hadith*), and the work of previous scholars and lawyers as a way of determining both law and religion.

DAILY PRAYER

As noted earlier, five particular duties are regarded as the minimum requirement of every Muslim. Termed the Five Pillars of Islam, they include the profession of one's faith in Allah as the one true god and in Muhammad as his prophet, almsgiving as a percentage of one's net worth, performing the *Hajj* once in one's lifetime, daily prayer, and fasting during the month of Ramadan. Every Muslim who is able to do so must perform these duties. Only those prevented by health, finances, or the well-being of their families are exempt. In the language of our analytical approach, these are Islam's five principal symbols.

With regard to daily prayer, Muslims orient themselves to God no less than five times a day through prayer: before dawn, noon, mid-afternoon, sunset, and just before nightfall. These prayers can be said in a large group, with family, or alone; they can be offered at work, at home, on vacation, or at school. Ideally they are said with fellow Muslims in a mosque, and for this reason Muslim men attend mosque on Fridays at noon.

The prayer itself follows a specific routine that is based on the example of the Prophet. It requires one to face in the direction of Mecca and stand, bow, kneel, and prostrate oneself before God while reciting praises and blessings to Him. Prostrating oneself before Allah is a physical act of complete submission. It is accomplished from a kneeling position by placing both hands flat on the ground in front of oneself and touching one's forehead to the ground. The word "mosque" means a "place of prostration."

Due to the demands of modern life, illness, or countless other reasons, no Muslim can find time for the performance of these prayers five times a day, each and every day of his or her life. Nonetheless, Muslims have the religious duty to try. This means that they sometimes have to combine prayers, perform an abbreviated version of the prayer, or make up for missed prayers at a later date. As individuals who have submitted their lives unconditionally to God, each Muslim is expected to hold himself or herself accountable to God for these prayers.

THE FAST OF RAMADAN

The Fast of Ramadan is another of the Five Pillars of Islam. It requires Muslims to abstain from all foods and liquids during the daylight hours of Ramadan, the ninth month of the Islamic year. Life in Islamic communities necessarily slows down during this month. This is especially true in the summer, when days

Facing Mecca in Prayer. For daily prayer a Muslim must face in the direction of Mecca to be properly oriented to God. In mosques, the direction of Mecca is often indicated by (a) a niche in the wall; otherwise, (b) lines on the floor can be used to indicate how adherents should align themselves for prayer. (Will Deming)

get long and hot. Since Muslims use a lunar calendar, this month "rotates" through the seasons on a thirty-three-year cycle.

Ramadan is a time when Muslims reflect on what is really necessary in life. It is a time to separate the things of Allah from *shirk* and to withdraw from the

"Thou hast authority, either
To punish them or
To treat them with kindness."

87. He said: "Whoever doth wrong,
Him shall we punish; then
Shall he be sent back
To his Lord; and He will
Punish him with a punishment
Unheard-of before.

88. "But whoever believes,
And works righteousness,–
He shall have a goodly
Reward, and easy will be
His task as we order it
By our command."

89. Then followed he another way,

90. Until, when he came
To the rising of the sun,
He found it rising
On a people for whom

قَالَ أَمَّا مَن ظَلَمَ فَسَوْفَ نُعَذِّبُهُ ثُمَّ يُرَدُّ إِلَىٰ رَبِّهِ فَيُعَذِّبُهُ عَذَابًا نُّكْرًا ۝

وَأَمَّا مَنْ ءَامَنَ وَعَمِلَ صَٰلِحًا فَلَهُ جَزَآءً الْحُسْنَىٰ وَسَنَقُولُ لَهُۥ مِنْ أَمْرِنَا يُسْرًا ۝

ثُمَّ أَتْبَعَ سَبَبًا ۝

حَتَّىٰٓ إِذَا بَلَغَ مَطْلِعَ الشَّمْسِ وَجَدَهَا تَطْلُعُ عَلَىٰ قَوْمٍ لَّمْ نَجْعَل لَّهُم مِّن دُونِهَا سِتْرًا ۝

(a)

The Qur'an. The message delivered by Muhammad is recorded in the Qur'an, which Muslims consider to be the very words of God, spoken in Arabic. For this reason, there are no "official" translations of the Qur'an into English or any other language, for all translations of the Qur'an are viewed as only aids for study, not the words of God. (a) When the Qur'an is translated into other languages, the Arabic is usually placed beside the translation.

(continued)

latter. It also provides Muslims an opportunity to reflect on the sufferings of the poor and reaffirm the place of the poor in God's society. For those outside Islam, the Fast of Ramadan and daily prayer are perhaps the most visible and arresting examples of how Muslims submit themselves to God as a means of orientation.

GUIDANCE AND AUTHORITY

Muslims, like Christians, hold several views as to how God communicates authoritatively with the profane world. Sunni Muslims, who number over one billion, make up the overwhelming majority of Muslims in the world today. In their understanding Muhammad is the culmination, or "seal," of the long history of God's prophets, a history that begins with Adam, the first man, and continues through Moses, the Hebrew prophets, and Jesus. Not only is his prophetic message held to be God's final and definitive statement to humanity, but Muhammad is seen as the foremost model of how a human being should respond to God. As a consequence, religious authority in the Sunni tradition derives primarily from the Qur'an and the many biographical reports (*hadith*) about

(b)

The Qur'an (continued). (b) Since it is the goal of every Muslim to become acquainted with Muhammad's message in the original, the interior and exterior walls of a mosque are often used to display important excerpts from the Qur'an in Arabic. Here verses from the Qur'an are inscribed on a minaret, the tower from which a mosque issues its call to prayer. (Will Deming)

Muhammad collected after his death, not an ongoing tradition of revelation. Sunnis have understood their religious leaders as "wise successors" to Muhammad and as religious scholars, not divinely inspired teachers; and Sunni religious scholars, or *ulemas*, are essentially laypersons who function as jurists of divine law (*sharia*). Their task is to clarify the meaning of the Qur'an on the basis of the *hadith* and the legal rulings of their predecessors. They have no special "holiness" or relationship vis-à-vis God.

In other types of Islam, however, Muslims have a different view of divine authority. Shiite Muslims, who number some 170 million, hold that prophecy did not stop with Muhammad. While the Qur'an is God's perfect and immutable message to humanity, God has spoken since Muhammad through inspired leaders who have both interpreted the Qur'an and supplemented its message with an authority equal to Muhammad's. For this reason, Shiites generally refer to their authority figures as "inspired leaders" (*imams*), rather than wise successors. The first of these inspired leaders was Ali, the Prophet's cousin and son-in-law, followed by his sons, Hasan and Husayn. Today Shiites live in expectation of a future inspired leader, whom they call the Mahdi, or "divinely guided

Islam's Prophetic Tradition. While most Muslims see Muhammad as God's final messenger to humanity, a sizable minority orient themselves to God through the message of prophets who have appeared after Muhammad. Most of these adherents remain within Islam, being seen by mainline Muslims as "heterodox" or "sectarian." The Baha'i religion is an example of a group that broke away from Islam over the issue of prophetic authority. Its prophet, Baha'u'llah, claimed that the prophets of all world religions speak with an authority comparable to Muhammad's. The Baha'i emblem is a nine-pointed star, which indicates the multiplicity of possible orientations to God. (Will Deming)

one." When the Ayatollah Khomeini came to power in Iran in 1979, many hoped that he would turn out to be this Mahdi.

By contrast, in Ahmadiyya Islam (about eight million adherents), Muslims believe that the Mahdi has already come. He is Mirza Ghulam Ahmad of India, who, near the end of the nineteenth century, proclaimed himself to be a reappearance of Muhammad, as well as Mahdi, messiah, and *avatar* of Vishnu. While Ahmadis regard the Qur'an as God's inspired message, their understanding of the Qur'an is determined by the revelations of their founder.

Some twenty years before this, in the 1860s, a man calling himself Baha'u'llah ("the glory of Allah") founded the Baha'i religion (about 7.1 million adherents). Baha'u'llah became convinced that he was the Mahdi who had been foretold by his teacher, a heterodox Shiite known as the Bab, or "the Gate" to true orientation. Following the teachings of these two prophetic leaders, Baha'is call for a unified world religion, whose vision of ultimate reality draws from all the sacred scriptures of the world. In Baha'i services it is common to hear readings from the Qur'an, as well as from the Bible, the *Bhagavadgita*, the Hindu *Laws of Manu*, the Buddhist *Dhammapada*, and the Zoroastrian *Avesta*, in addition to the writings of the Bab, Baha'u'llah, and Abdu'l-Baha, the latter's son. Baha'is believe that all of these contain authoritative insights as to how people should orient themselves to God.

chapter 9

Primal Religions

"Primal religions" is a designation scholars use to describe small tribal or indigenous traditions of orientation to ultimate reality. In the past they have also gone under the names "primitive religions" or "little traditions" (as opposed to the "great traditions"). Depending on the criteria one uses to define primal religions, they encompass anywhere from one hundred to three hundred million adherents and are found in all parts of the globe, in both rural and urban areas. A basic list of primal religions would include the religions of Eskimos, Native Americans, and the eighty or so distinct peoples of South America; the religions of the sixty or so tribal peoples of Africa; and the indigenous religions of Siberia, Australia, and the South Pacific Islands. It might also include several religious traditions in the subcultures of East Asian countries (for example, Chinese folk traditions).

Because primal religions encompass a plurality of religious traditions rather than a single tradition, like Buddhism or Islam, our approach in this chapter will differ from the previous chapters in this part. Instead of examining specific symbols and visions of ultimate reality, we will focus on five broad patterns of orientation that are common among primal religions. Since these religions are small and mostly unfamiliar to Western readers, this approach seems more suited to an introductory treatment. Thus, rather than discussing orientation to Peritnalík, the creator god of the Tobas of South America, or the ritual importance of sweet potatoes among the Venda of southeast Africa, we will look at:

- The connectedness of the different realities in primal religions
- Religious leadership
- Symbols that put one at the center
- Higher realities understood as power
- Transcending profane reality through ordeals

THE CONNECTEDNESS OF ALL REALITY

Most primal traditions see reality—profane, ultimate, and higher-order realities—as an interconnected whole. It is a "grand economy" in which each element has a rightful place, and from this place must interact with, give deference to, and support the other elements for the harmonious working of the whole. Anthropologists often refer to this as a "holistic" approach to the world, as opposed to the "fragmented" or "diversified" worldview they find in modern societies.

Because of the interconnectedness of all things, orientation to ultimate reality, whether envisioned as a god, gods, or a spirit world, involves keeping up relations, so to speak, with representatives from other realms. By endowing animals, plants, rocks, rivers, the sky, and the land with souls, a practice scholars call "animism," primal religions envision the world as alive and communicative in a way it is not in other religions. Thus, speaking with Raven, or Tiger, or Elk might be necessary for keeping up with the needs and expectations of the forest creatures. Before hunting season a tribal leader might hold a feast for Bear or Seal to honor his "people," thank them for their sacrifice, or apologize for the necessity of human beings impinging on their world. Likewise, vegetal spirits and weather-related phenomena (Goddess Moon, Sun, Wind Spirit) are consulted when crops are planted, tended, and harvested.

Appeasing the Spirit World. The wholeness that adherents of primal religions sense in their world often obligates them to placate gods or spirits for encroaching on their realms. After this eagle was killed for its feathers, a Sarsi tribesman of Saskatchewan holds it in his left hand and performs a ceremony designed to appease the eagle spirits. His right hand holds a rattle by which he gains the attention of the spirit world. (Photo by Edward S. Curtis, *The North American Indian*, vol. 18, plate 634)

Ancestors, especially, need symbolic attention. They are the unseen half of human society, without which neither the family nor the community can be complete. Usually this means they must receive honor for their past deeds, and they must be fed. These symbolic acts are accomplished by recounting legends in which they are the heroes, associating them with landmarks and grave sites, inviting them to feasts, and leaving food out for them on a special shelf or stand. Ancestors also live closer to the gods or spirit world than the part of humanity that remains in the profane world. Favorable interaction with them is therefore a way to orient oneself to other higher-order realities.

It is out of this concern for the ancestors that primal religions often have elaborate end-of-life rituals. The way in which older members of the community are treated in final days of life, and the way in which they are buried or cremated, assures their passage into the next existence. If something should go wrong—if a cremation fire goes out or a corpse is turned in the wrong direction—the harmony of the whole is threatened. An ancestor might enter the next world as a troubled or vengeful spirit, provoking the indignation of the gods. By the same token, primal religions often have elaborate birth rituals. These symbolic actions provide safe passage to those coming into profane reality from another realm.

RELIGIOUS LEADERS

A tribe or group's participation in the harmonious workings of the cosmos is often orchestrated by religious professionals. These are known variously as priests, shamans, witch doctors, medicine men, and mediums. Their job is to mediate between their people and the unseen world of the spirits and gods, to serve as technicians who maintain cosmic balance. They invite representatives of the unseen world to take part in celebrations held in their honor, they offer gifts for the well-being of their people, and they supervise rituals designed to appease angry gods and spirits. These religious leaders also serve their people as a repository of sacred knowledge. They instruct the sick in the use of herbal medicines and higher-order powers of healing; they pass down authoritative mythologies, such as creation stories; and they initiate adherents into new orientations to ultimate reality through various rites of passage.

These priests and shamans have these capabilities because they nurture special connections with higher realities. They undergo ecstatic experiences, such as possessions and spiritual journeys, that bring them face-to-face with the unseen world, and they endear themselves to various messengers, or "spirit familiars," who travel between profane reality and other realms. These include birds, who provide information from an aerial and heavenly vantage point; snakes, who have knowledge of the world below; and other creatures thought to have esoteric knowledge of the cosmos.

Shamans. Religious leaders in primal religions maintain their authority by developing special relations with higher-order realities. This medicine man (shaman) orients himself to the power and wisdom of the animal world by wearing a ceremonial bear skin. (Photo by Edward S. Curtis, *The North American Indian*, vol. 5, plate 150)

SYMBOLS OF THE CENTER

From their vision of the cosmos as a connected whole, adherents of primal religions often seek out symbols that orient them to ultimate reality by positioning them at the "center" of all reality. Sometimes poles are used to mark or establish this center. These can be poles in the middle of a village or sacred precinct or the central support pole of a dwelling. Because it takes place at the center of reality, life lived close to these poles is more real and meaningful than life elsewhere in the profane world.

As a vertical object that rises into the heavens, a pole can also function as an "axis," connecting profane reality with higher realities. In this way it becomes an important tool for communication between the realities, or even a point for crossing over between them. During religious ceremonies gods and spirits can use these poles to descend into our reality to partake of human hospitality or to "take possession" of someone by entering into his or her body. Adherents, in turn, use these poles to channel wisdom into the profane world from other realms, and on occasion they follow the pole upward on a journey into the world of the spirits.

Aside from using poles, adherents of primal religions also envision time in a way that puts them at the center. Instead of being linear or historical, as in modern societies, time in these religions is primarily cyclical—beginning, ending, and beginning again each year. This is not to say that adherents of primal

(a)

(b)

(c)

Masks and Totems. Playing the part of animals and birds in ceremonial dances and honoring them with large carved images are two important ways that adherents of primal religions maintain close relations with the unseen world. Shown here are (a) a dancer dressed as a mythical bird (that is, a bird from another reality); (b) a totem pole honoring an eagle and a grizzly bear; and (c) the head of a raven, whose beak opens to give entrance to a place of worship. (Photos by Edward S. Curtis, *The North American Indian*, vol. 10, plates 336, 330, and 350)

Symbols of the Center. Poles and trees are used to locate the "center" of reality as well as provide a point of contact between realms. A medicine fraternity of the Arikara tribe of North Dakota gathers in front of a cedar that serves this function. (Photo by Edward S. Curtis, *The North American Indian*, vol. 5, plate 164)

religions have *no* concept of linear time, no experience of aging or memory of past generations. Rather, they have a different emphasis. In these religions people find more meaning in things that happen again and again than in the unique, solitary events of linear history. The seasons, the cycle of procreation, the time of the hunt or the harvest: These are integrated into the sacred economy of the cosmos in a way that a particular military victory of a certain tribal chief sometime in the past can never be.

Consequently, adherents of primal religions harmonize their lives with such things as the cycles of the moon and the end and beginning of the year. They focus on what, for them, is the essence or reality of time. In this way they are able to conform the monthly and yearly routines of life to cosmic patterns and eternal archetypes. Hunting and planting crops are no longer short-lived, profane activities, but timeless symbolic acts that connect human life with ultimate meaning and purpose.

ULTIMATE REALITY AND POWER

Primal religions envision ultimate reality in a variety of ways: as a spirit world, as a single great spirit, or as a group of gods, sometimes under the informal leadership of a principal god. Rarely is ultimate reality structured or organized to the degree that it is in the other religious traditions we have considered. Anthropologists have attributed this aspect of primal religions to the fact that these religions exist mostly in oral cultures. Without a sustained, written record of theological inquiry, systematic theology does not develop beyond a certain stage. Likewise, primal religions generally lack a theologian who can articulate his or her religion to outsiders.

This explanation may, indeed, be correct. From our analytical perspective, however, we can at least conclude that systematic speculation is not an important symbol in primal religions. As a consequence, the adherents of primal re-

Controlling Menacing Powers. Taboo avoidance and purification rites keep adherents of primal religions safe from the dangers of the spirit world. Here a whale hunter covers himself with hemlock branches and undergoes an elaborate washing ritual to make himself pleasing to the whale spirit. (Photo by Edward S. Curtis, *The North American Indian*, vol. 11, plate 370)

ligions often understand ultimate reality as a realm of relatively undifferentiated beings, sustained by a common, underlying power. Since no god or spirit has a clear monopoly on this power, orientation becomes more an activity of coming to terms with this power than nurturing a relationship with a particular god or spirit. The important religious questions are often: Who presently controls this power, and how can we best deal with him or her?

In line with this, the symbols of primal religions include not only various methods for honoring and appeasing higher-order beings, but also a full array of magical practices designed to manipulate them or ward them off. Taboo restrictions, for example, are fairly common in primal religions. These offer protection through the avoidance of things that make humans vulnerable to higher-order realities. Similarly, purifications are a way to remove the taint of these things after a person has come into contact with them. Knowledge of certain numbers and sequences can also keep one out of harm's way. These can define safe quantities and correct procedures in activities that involve danger, such as hunting. Finally, certain objects can be imbued with power from the spirit world, thereby serving as symbolic tools called "fetishes." These can be weapons for the hunt or objects used in rituals, such as musical instruments, rattles, and masks.

A Ritual Rattle. Objects used in rituals are often thought to possess powers or spirits from another reality. Here a shaman holds an empowered rattle in his right hand, which he uses for calling various representatives of the spirit world to him. In his left hand he holds the tribe's speaker staff, which allows one to speak openly in the tribal assembly. (Photo by Edward S. Curtis, *The North American Indian*, vol. 10, plate 333)

ORDEALS

The desire to control the power of the unseen world also leads to the practice of ordeals in primal religions. These are activities that push a human being to his or her limits, both physically and emotionally. They include prolonged isolation from the community, fasting and bloodletting, and subjecting oneself to the extremes of bitter cold or intense heat. The purpose of undertaking an ordeal is to move oneself beyond the limitations of the profane world. By dominating one's world through superhuman feats, one can cross over into a higher-order reality and realize new possibilities for taking control of one's life.

In the tribal religions of North America, for instance, both men and women spend time in "sweat lodges." These are closed structures with a fire pit in the middle. Coals and hot stones are placed in this pit, raising the temperature of the lodge to the point where the participants in the ritual sweat profusely. Ample drinking water is provided, enabling them to continue perspiring without becoming dehydrated. This is understood as a cleansing ordeal, which allows them to gain a purity that will harmonize them with the spiritual world.

More often than not, ordeals are undertaken as part of a rite of passage. A girl just beginning menstruation, for example, might spend days or weeks in an isolation hut, so that she will be properly oriented to the spirit world when she attains womanhood. Likewise, aspiring warriors and hunters must undergo ordeals of isolation out in the forest or jungle. Here, through hunger-induced visions, they establish their first communications with important representatives of the animal world.

Becoming a shaman or tribal priest can even require ordeals that bring a person close to death. In some primal religions, aspiring shamans must become extremely sick, a feat that gives them access to the spirit world in the same way that a dying person enters it. In Siberia, for example, young shamans challenge each other to blanket-drying contests. In preparation for the ordeal, they consume large quantities of spicy foods and drink the juice of a hallucinogenic mushroom. On the day of the competition, they stand knee-deep in snow while older shamans place wet blankets on their bare upper bodies. Their goal is to produce enough body heat to dry more blankets than their competitors. As each blanket dries, it is replaced with a new wet one. After this ordeal, the participants are feverish, weak, and dehydrated and must undergo long periods of recovery. It is during this time that they receive the visions that initiate them into the higher mysteries of their profession.

PART THREE

COMPLEXITIES, LIMITS, ETHICS

⊰chapter 10⊱

CHANGE IN SYMBOLIC SYSTEMS OVER TIME

In part two we saw many examples of how *symbols*, understood as tools for orientation to ultimate reality, function within *religions*, understood as systems for
such orientation. For the purpose of that discussion we treated religions by and
large as static entities, frozen in a particular moment in time. But religions change
over time, sometimes radically. Symbols take on new meanings or are eclipsed
by other symbols, and visions of profane reality, higher-order realities, and ultimate reality change as well. Examples of this abound and account for the rich
diversity of religious traditions in human history. Within Christianity, for example, three principal branches have emerged in the course of history—Roman
Catholic, Orthodox, and Protestant—each encompassing multiple schools, denominations, fellowships, orders, and sects. Each of these, in turn, has formulated its own understanding of the different realities and of what constitutes the
appropriate tools for orientation. As one might suppose, this aspect of religion
makes the task of analysis more complex. In this chapter, consequently, we will
consider how we, as students of religion, can best account for change in religions over time.

We should perhaps first note that religious adherents often accord little or no
importance to changes in their own religions. While major renewal movements
in a tradition's history may be understood as the beginning of a new era (or
"age," "epoch," or "dispensation"), for most people the idea of *ultimate* reality
argues against seeing one's own religion as a dynamic system in continual flux.
Since Christians, for example, consider Jesus Christ to be "the same yesterday,
today, and forever," it stands to reason that the means of orienting oneself to
him will not change from year to year.

By contrast, standard textbook treatments of religion often *emphasize*
change, especially change occasioned by historical circumstances. Transformations in a religious tradition are understood as arising from social and political
upheaval, technological advance, and cultural borrowing. Yet if our goal is to
understand the distinctively *religious* dimensions of change in a religious tradition, this common and seemingly straightforward approach is inadequate.
While it can lead to a better understanding of history's role in a religion, or a

religion's role in history, its focus on historical causality tends to distract us from the religion's own inner dynamic.

Let us reflect, by analogy, on literary criticism. Few, I think, would be satisfied with an account of the development of a literary tradition if it consisted primarily of an analysis of the historical factors (political, economic, etc.) that influenced its various authors. While these events cannot be ignored, such an undertaking must first and foremost be guided by an appreciation for literature per se. Inasmuch as we recognize a distinctively *literary* dimension to human life—a discrete "world" of literature—the dynamics of a literary tradition will not be fathomed by reference to historical factors alone. So too with art, so too with music, so too with religion. The proper starting point for analyzing religious change, therefore, is not a tradition's historical context. It is an appreciation of religion per se. Only in this way can we ascertain what is distinctively religious in the course of a religion's development.

Given what we have said in previous chapters, an analytical appreciation of religion will, at minimum, include the recognition that every religious tradition is a coherent *system*, intelligible in terms of its own inner-logic. This leads us to two fundamental insights for analysis. First, by virtue of the system's coherency, a change, even a subtle one, in one aspect of a religion—say, its understanding of a symbol—will result in a "compensating" change in another— for example, a new use for that symbol. And second, knowledge of a religion's inner-logic will enable one, in some measure, to anticipate the nature of this compensating change. To get a sense of how these insights contribute to the work of analysis, we will examine two examples of religious change already familiar to many readers.

EXAMPLE ONE: THE INNOVATIONS OF MARTIN LUTHER

As a young friar in the Roman Catholic tradition, Martin Luther, the reputed father of the Protestant Reformation, felt overwhelmed by the symbols of his religion. The more he tried to orient himself to God using prayer, confession, and penance, the more he became aware of his *dis*orientation from ultimate reality—his "sinfulness." In our language of analysis, Luther found the symbolic system of the Roman Catholic tradition ineffective. Given his vision of profane and ultimate reality, these tools were "inappropriate."

Through his study of Saint Augustine, the Psalms, and the letters of Saint Paul, Luther attempted to resolve this situation by introducing a change into his religious tradition: He began to re-envision ultimate reality. Rather than understand ultimate reality as a God whose quality of moral perfection, or "righteousness," created an enormous gulf between profane and ultimate reality, Luther began to envision ultimate reality as a God who offered this righteousness to his adherents in the profane world, making them more like ultimate re-

(a)

(b)

Sola Scriptura, *"Scripture Alone." Following Luther's rejection of the Roman Catholic hierarchy as a source of religious authority, he and other Protestants promoted the Bible as the final arbitrator of proper orientation to God. As a result, Bible study has become a central symbol in many Protestant traditions, even to the extent that (a) children attend "vacation Bible school" (VBS) in the summer, and (b) some Protestant colleges identify their courses of study as "Bible based."* (Will Deming)

ality. It was thus the activity of ultimate reality that provided the basis for orientation, not the (symbolic) activities of human beings.

Eventually Luther formulated this new vision of ultimate reality as a God who saved people by "grace," through their "faith in Jesus Christ." Translating this into our analytic language, Luther's understanding of ultimate reality led him to declare that orientation through belief in a particular manifestation of God (God the Son) brought about the desired relationship with ultimate reality. Hence, faith took its place as a primary symbol in Luther's religion.

From these initial changes to the inner-logic and symbolic system of Roman Catholicism, there ensued further, "compensating" changes. By promoting faith as the necessary and sufficient tool for proper orientation (*sola fides*, "faith alone"), Luther and his followers came to deny both the appropriateness of other Catholic symbols as well as the Catholic understanding of higher-order realities. Devotion to the Virgin Mary and the saints was denounced, as was the clergy's role as intermediary between God and the profane world. The clergy's exclusive access to the wine of the eucharist was censured; and celibacy for priests, monks, and nuns as a means of securing privileged positions vis-à-vis ultimate reality was condemned. This diminished status of the clergy led Luther to identify the Bible as the highest source of religious authority, above the church hierarchy and its ecclesiastical tradition (*sola scriptura*, "scripture alone"). As a result, Lutherans promoted biblical interpretation as an important symbol, both for clergy and laity. In turn, preaching—the public exposition of Scripture—became a powerful tool whereby clergy oriented Christians and non-Christians alike to ultimate reality.

EXAMPLE TWO: WOMEN'S CHANGING ROLE IN MODERN JUDAISM

Nowadays it is frequently observed that most religions are male-centered, or "androcentric," meaning that men play the primary role in orienting themselves and others to ultimate reality. While women participate in religions, their relation to ultimate reality is usually mediated by men. This is by no means a new observation, and instances of androcentrism in religion are unambiguous and legion. Indeed, the vast majority of the world's religious adherents still relate to ultimate reality through religious hierarchies that are, in their uppermost ranks, exclusively male.

Especially in the closing decades of the twentieth century, advocates of women's liberation and feminism have become important voices in religion, with the result that nonandrocentric forms of traditional religions have begun to develop. In Judaism, which is the focus of this example, the Reform and Conservative traditions in particular have been influenced by this change. In contrast to more traditional forms of Judaism, such as Orthodox Judaism, in which only men can be rabbis, these groups now ordain both men and women. Consistent with this new understanding of who can mediate between profane and ultimate realities, these traditions also promote the practice of counting women among the *minyan*, or quorum of adults needed to hold a prayer service. In both cases, appropriate orientation to God has been redefined: It is now something that adult females may orchestrate with the same authority as adult males.

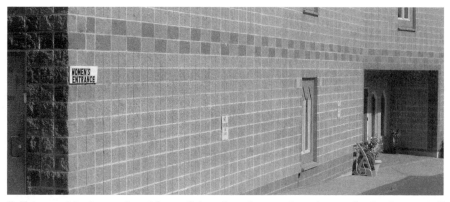

Religion and Androcentrism. Most religions have been and continue to be "androcentric," giving principle leadership roles to men rather than women. Many have predominantly (or exclusively) male priesthoods, and women adherents are cordoned off, theologically and socially, to their own separate spaces. It is not uncommon, for example, for mosques to have separate entrances for women. (Will Deming)

In line with these changes, new tools for orientation have been adopted for girls. As the counterpart to the circumcision of male babies, a service of prayer and blessing for female babies has become popular. Even more common is the *bat mitzvah*, which is the female equivalent of the traditional *bar mitzvah*. With

Daughters of the Commandment. This youth director at a Conservative synagogue is one of many women in Judaism taking a leading role in her religion. She directs morning prayer wearing items traditionally reserved for men: the prayer shawl (tallit), *the leather phylacteries* (tefillin) *on her forehead and right arm, and a head covering* (yarmulke), *which for women is often jeweled.* (Will Deming)

this ceremony a girl attains her "majority" (adult status) within the religious community. She becomes a "daughter of the commandment," preparing the way for her to participate in the liturgy of the synagogue.

In both these examples we see that changes made to some of the elements in a religious tradition lead to changes in others, by virtue of these elements all participating in a coherent symbolic *system*. Naturally, both examples could be fleshed out in greater detail. If we were to do so, we could delineate with even more precision the specifically *religious* dynamics of these important changes in Christianity and Judaism.

≼chapter 11≽

FURTHER COMPLEXITIES OF ANALYSIS

As we have formulated it thus far, the analysis of religions is a process of identifying a religion's various (and changing) elements—its symbols, its visions of profane, higher-order, and ultimate realities—and determining the "inner-logic" that holds these together in a coherent system. Symbols function in the way they do—as tools for orientation—by taking part in the larger system of meaning that is particular to a religion. It is imperative, therefore, to keep this system of meaning in view.

This is satisfactory for an initial description, but there is more. It should come as no surprise that the attempt to understand a human activity as old and ubiquitous as "orientation to ultimate reality" will run afoul of any introductory guidelines. The purpose of this chapter is to move beyond these basics and reflect on some of the complexities and challenges that await the intermediate and advanced student of religion. It will also provide a caution against the sorts of misconceptions and facile conclusions that one so frequently finds in the analysis of religion.

THE CENTRAL CHALLENGE

Let us begin with what is perhaps the most daunting and, at the same time, the most exciting challenge of analyzing religions. To be successful, one must be able to piece together a way of thinking—a "logic"—alien to one's own worldview or sensibilities. Because *anything* can function as a symbol, and because visions of profane, higher-order, and ultimate realities can differ radically among religions, the inner-logic of a religion may take us into worldviews that we never imagined existed. To meet this challenge, one must avoid the common error of assuming, however tacitly, that the inner-logic of a religion will bear some resemblance to his or her own notion of logical thought. Take the following illustration:

93

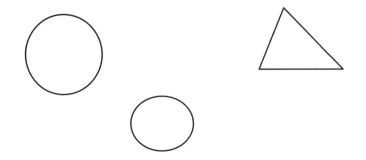

Which of these shapes belong together? The "obvious" answer for most of us would be the circles. This is, after all, how we measure a person's IQ in our society. But this might not be obvious to others. Perhaps the answer is the larger circle and the triangle because they are uppermost on the page. Or perhaps it is these two precisely *because* they are different, and therefore "balanced" in some perspective. Or maybe it *is* the circles, but not because they are the same shape, but because they were both drawn by Zen masters and offer a glimpse of enlightenment.

Religious notions of "clean" and "unclean" provide a second example. In Judaism, pork and eel are unclean foods; in Hinduism, sandal-making and fishing are unclean occupations, while bathing in the Ganges, one of India's most polluted rivers, is cleansing. Clearly the "logics" operating in these two religions are not those of modern germ theory, and any attempt to devise an explanation in those terms ("pork carries disease") only obscures the matter. Likewise, it gets us nowhere to conclude that these religions are "confused" or "illogical." Mov-

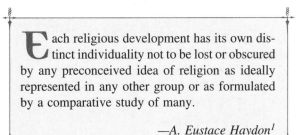

> Each religious development has its own distinct individuality not to be lost or obscured by any preconceived idea of religion as ideally represented in any other group or as formulated by a comparative study of many.
>
> —A. Eustace Haydon[1]

ing from an admission—"it makes no sense to me"—to the judgment—"it makes no sense"—is almost always regrettable. It is the same error that tourists make when trying to "make sense of" another culture.

What is required in these cases, happily, is not despair, but patience and good, old-fashioned detective work. One needs to "tease out" a religion's inner-logic from the evidence through close observation and native intuition. The difficulty in understanding symbols is almost always a reflection of one's ignorance of their participation in a larger system of meaning. Unless one knows the biblical criteria for unclean animals, and that these also include rabbit, camel, and rock badger, it is impossible to understand the symbolic logic of the biblical prohibition against pork. Likewise, one needs to know that *all* occupations in Hinduism are unclean to members of other classes and castes and that, aside from being water, which often suggests itself as a symbol for cleansing, the Ganges is a Goddess and a consort of Shiva, and its headwaters are said to originate in heaven and flow through Shiva's hair before touching the earth.

THE KNOWLEDGE OF INSIDERS

This last example illustrates another point: The relation of a symbol to its larger religious system can be manifold and complex. In fact, the major symbols in a religion are always "multivalent." They mean several things simultaneously, even to a single person. If one were to ask Christians about the meaning of baptism or Buddhists about the effects of meditation, one would receive more answers than persons asked. It is the nature of symbols that they strike human sensibilities deeply, broadly, and variously.

And with this observation comes a caution: One should never assume that the members of a particular religion can explain that religion's inner-logic. Given the multivalence of symbols, insiders can provide only individual perspectives on their religions—"what my religion means to me." Further, it is often the case that insiders know *nothing* of a religion from an analytic perspective. If allowed to reason from their own impressions of what is "obvious," insiders can be a rich source of *mis*information.

"Insiders," we must remember, are such because they *use* symbols for orientation, not because they understand the rationale behind these symbols. What they know most often is only that these, and not other things, "work," for a symbol's efficacy rarely depends on a knowledge of *how* it works. For example, it is difficult to find a Roman Catholic who can explain the former practice of abstaining from meat on Friday or a Muslim who knows the symbolic logic for kissing the black stone in Mecca. That these are symbols is evident. How they work is not. What most Roman Catholics and Muslims know is that these symbols are (or were) important and necessary. An analysis such as we are considering here is as foreign to them as the workings of the internal combustion engine are to the average motorist.

> The study of religion has rarely amounted to more than a reporter repeating the insider's unsubstantiated claims.
>
> —*Russell McCutcheon*[2]

Let us consider an analogy from the world of market research. Consumerism, like religion, is an activity. Like "orientation to ultimate reality," buying, using, reusing, recycling, and disposing of products can be analyzed into patterns of behavior governed by an inner-logic. Naturally, it behooves the providers of goods and services to inform themselves of these patterns—the desires, needs, values, and expectations of the "practitioner," the consumer. When they do so, however, it is not by asking consumers directly, as in, "Please tell us what you want so we can supply it." Rather, they hire experts in market research. These experts collect data through carefully designed survey instruments, such as telephone questionnaires and focus groups, and then analyze it.

The assumption that underlies this expensive undertaking is that consumers are not capable of market analysis. While there may be method in their consumption, they are unable to articulate its inner-logic directly to a manufacturer. Instead, their judgments about what they want and why must be collected and studied by those who have made market analysis their field of expertise.

What necessitates market research are the simple observations that there is a difference between what people want and what they say they want and that being a consumer does not guarantee that one is knowledgeable about or even conscious of the mechanics of consumption. In the same way, students of religion must recognize that religious people are, with few exceptions, incapable of articulating *how* their religions work. The exceptions include intellectuals, scholars, and theologians. Otherwise, the vast majority of religious adherents, like consumers, are essential sources of raw data; but this data needs analysis, which they cannot supply.

REASSESSING OUR NOTION OF "INNER-LOGIC"

As stated earlier, we have stressed the importance of understanding a religion as a coherent system defined by an "inner-logic." Consistent with this, we have described change as a process by which the elements of a religion wax and wane and develop, all within this idyllically coherent system. Yet consider the following anecdote:

> In ancient China, a family feeds the ancestral spirits by setting out a bowl of rice and some choice pieces of duck before retiring for bed. They also take the precaution of tying up the family cat so it will not eat the duck. Three or four generations later, descendants of the family continue these practices, but begin to lose sight of the rationale behind them. They tie up the cat and put out the rice, knowing only that these things are the traditional ways of serving the spirit world. After the eighth generation, descendants of the same family, equally devout, simply tie up the cat.

As this anecdote makes clear, religious systems are not fully coherent, nor are the elements of a religion always informed by a single inner-logic. In our anecdote, the initial inner-logic—namely, that the ancestors are a link to ultimate reality, that they experience hunger, and that one can ingratiate oneself to them by rice offerings—has been disrupted by something as serendipitous as human forgetfulness. Tying up the cat, an incidental part of the original ritual, is now the symbol of choice, with no inner-logic in sight. Furthermore, had this anecdote not been of our own invention, we would not even be in a position to postulate why this was so.

If the truth be told, a whole range of things regularly "intrudes upon" and "disrupts" the coherence of religious systems, introducing small idiosyncrasies as well as entirely new features into a tradition. These "intrusions" are things like theological creativity and borrowing, cultural influences, and political events. Under theological creativity, for example, we could list Nietzsche's declaration that "God is dead" or Mahatma Gandhi's promotion of *satyagraha* ("holding on to truth"), which became the basis of India's passive resistance movement. For theological borrowing, we need only reflect on the influence that Buddhism has had on American Christianity in the past fifty years. Moving beyond an initial fascination with Buddhist techniques of meditation, some Christian groups now organize interfaith dialogues with Buddhist communities.

Cultural influences, in turn, are evident in the differences between forms of the same religion as practiced in distinct cultures. Thus, Balinese Hinduism uses the symbols of tooth-filing and rice cultivation, which are unknown among Hindus in India; and even Judaism in Manhattan's Upper West Side is distinct from its cousin in nearby Rhode Island. Finally, political events can include things like the Maurya dynasty's patronage of Buddhism in the third century BC and the Emperor Constantine's endorsement of Christianity in the fourth century AD. Both these events transformed marginal groups into mainstream religions, bringing about dramatic changes in their symbolic structures. Yet political events can also include catastrophes, such as the Holocaust. This horrific act of genocide caused disjunctures in the inner-logic of Judaism so profound that questions as basic as "Who is God?" and "Can one still be a Jew?" guided many post-Holocaust theologies.

In sum, the exasperating, disorderly, and exciting fact facing intermediate and advanced students of religion is this: No religion is explicable in terms of a single inner-logic. Religions are always eclectic systems in which several inner-logics are at play. They harbor vestiges, layers, and accumulations from earlier periods, the meanings of which are often lost in the shadows of history and resist analysis of any sort.

Yet, there is also a positive side to such blessed chaos. While this reassessment of a religion's "inner-logic" adds a new level of complexity to analysis, it also brings clarity to the classification of religious traditions. As a religion develops and changes over time, distinct emphases emerge. When this happens, the inner-logics that come to dominate a tradition determine its boundaries: Christianity as opposed to Hinduism, or Islam as opposed to primal religions. In addition, the less important or secondary logics at work in a tradition determine its various "species" (for example, Catholic, Orthodox, and Protestant Christianity), and "subspecies" (for example, Episcopalian, Methodist,

(a)

(b)

(c)

Cultural Influences. As religions spread from culture to culture, their symbols are sometimes interpreted and developed by the receiving cultures in radically new ways. When Buddhism came to China in the first and early second centuries AD, many Chinese theologians envisioned the Buddha as (a) a fat, jolly sage rather than (b) the austere figure that had developed in early Indian Buddhism and was accepted by most other cultures. In some cases the religious symbols of two cultures are combined, as in (c) this facade of Our Lady of Vietnam Catholic Church. Here the Christian cross is combined with Asian architecture, ceremonial gong, and a diagram of the cosmic forces Yin and Yang. (Will Deming)

Southern Baptist). These latter are what we call "denominations," "schools," and "sects."

As religions continue to develop, new species and subspecies appear. Sometimes the outcome is an important revival or reform movement. At other times it is a "heresy" or a new religion altogether, as when Buddhism emerged from Hinduism, and Christianity from Judaism. When a religion's secondary logics diverge sharply from the leading logics of its principal tradition, we have what are called "fringe" groups. Examples of fringe groups associated with Christianity include Christian Science, the Latter-day Saints ("Mormons"), messianic Judaism ("Jews for Jesus," etc.), and Unitarians. Are these "Christian," and to what extent? This question really has no answer from an analytical perspective. Of the various logics that govern each of these traditions, some are arguably Christian, some are arguably not.

⊰chapter 12⊱

THE LIMITS OF ANALYSIS

In considering the complexities of analysis, we have already encountered one type of limitation: Symbols can lose their logical connection with their larger religious systems. When this happens they often continue on as part of the tradition, but become opaque or altogether obscure. The remarkable deference shown to cows in Hinduism, for example, has no good explanation. Here we are reminded that the only criterion for a symbol is that it is deemed appropriate by its tradition as a tool for orientation to ultimate reality. It need not "make sense" in any other way.

This type of limitation on analysis is essentially historical. Scholars do not have enough information about the development of most religions to sort out all the disruptions and changes in their inner-logics. A more fundamental limitation stems from the inherent dissimilarity between the act of analysis and the act of participating in a religion. Analysis, as we have defined it, seeks to identify and coordinate the elements of a religion—its symbols, its visions of the various realities, and the inner-logics that hold these together in a coherent system. Participation, by contrast, involves the *use* of symbols. These are fundamentally

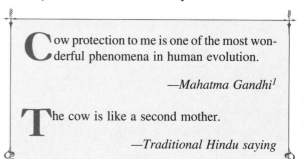

Cow protection to me is one of the most wonderful phenomenon in human evolution.

—Mahatma Gandhi[1]

The cow is like a second mother.

—Traditional Hindu saying

different "ways of knowing" a religion, and while they are not mutually exclusive, in practice they are seldom brought together in any significant way in the same person. Just as great art critics are rarely great artists, great students of religion are rarely great religious figures.

As a result, a very important aspect of religions, the *experiences* of the insider, will elude the analyst. This is always true when one studies a religion other than one's own, a matter we can illustrate by comparing religious experiences to experiences with new foods. In my classes there are always a few students who have never tasted a kiwi fruit. Even though their classmates have eaten many kiwis, the latter are never able to convey to the former what a kiwi

100

tastes like. Their descriptions sound like this: "A kiwi is a crunchy, hairy sort of fruit. It tastes something like a lemony banana." On the basis of such information the kiwi-deprived come no closer to understanding the experiences of the kiwi eaters, and no amount of discussion has ever helped. To gain this way of knowing for themselves, the kiwi-deprived must finally *taste* a kiwi.

Now, it is possible for an analyst to "taste" a religion that he or she is studying. But there is some limit, surely, to how many religions one person can join in a lifetime. And even when an analyst already belongs to the religion in question, there is no guarantee that his or her experiences are "normative." Symbols are multivalent, and the experiences of those who use them vary greatly.

> **B**ecause there are so many religious traditions and so many types of experience within those traditions, I look upon the quest for a neat, precise definition of "religious experience"—even a definition "for the purposes of this study"—as fruitless.
>
> —*Caroline Davis*[2]

Beyond this, even our example with the kiwi does not tell the whole story. Even though eating a kiwi may strike non-kiwi eaters as "exotic" or "foreign," it is nonetheless part of our mundane, material existence. Yet religious experiences presuppose *other* realities and are therefore one step beyond this sort of access. Joining a religion—orienting oneself to a religion's vision of ultimate reality—is not the same as tasting something new. It entails an extraordinary experience, something on the order of sensing a fourth dimension.

This is why those who participate in religions so often resort to "otherworldly" or "religious" language to describe their experiences. They use metaphors and negative definitions—"God is a vast ocean"; "His thoughts are not our thoughts." They describe "liminal" states of being and higher states of consciousness, and they communicate their experiences by way of paradox, inference, and what is left unsaid. Clearly, these are not the locutions of "analytical knowing," and it is difficult, if not impossible, to translate them into the language of analysis. To the extent that these experiences are linked with another reality, one can no more "explain" them in analytical terms than one can "explain" the sublime in music or literature. In these cases, *translatio traditio est:* Translation is betrayal.

> **T**he paradox, the linguistic impossibility, of words such as *absolute, transcendent,* or *infinite,* combined with their linguistic necessity, is the embarrassment of all religious language.
>
> —*Rita Gross*[3]

Another important difference between tasting a kiwi and experiencing ultimate reality is that the one is a limited encounter, the other is not. Ultimate reality, we must remember, is not just another, or a different, or even a higher reality. It is ultimate. *Infi-*

nite in scope, it is not only enigmatic, but *infinitely* so. This means that every insider's experience of ultimate reality is both unanalytical *and partial*. The sentiment, "The truth that can be fully known is not the truth," is universal among religions.

To illustrate this, let us recall our earlier model of the student of religion as someone who observes a building project (chapter 3). In that model we likened the analysis of religions to one person watching another person work on a project, the observer seeing the tools and actions of the worker, but not yet the object of the worker's labor. I proposed that the observer would nonetheless be able to piece together the goal of the worker on the basis of the latter's tools and actions. What this proposal assumes, however, is that the worker understands what he or she is striving for—the building of a wall or a patio—and acts accordingly. What I am now suggesting is that the success of this procedure of observation-and-hypothesis is, for the analysis of religions, limited by the fact that "the worker"—the religious adherent—does not fully comprehend the nature of the project because "the project"—orientation to ultimate reality—involves an element that is inscrutable to an infinite degree.

Ironically, this becomes more, not less, true as an adherent closes in on the object of his or her efforts. As one orients himself or herself more perfectly to ultimate reality—as one becomes "enlightened"—he or she moves away from the reality in which an analysis of this experience has any relevance or meaning. This is because analytical knowledge and religious experience are not only different ways of knowing, but also, at some point, antithetical. What insiders seek is "enlightenment," "wisdom," or "revelation," and this is never identical with erudition, intellectual understanding, or logical reasoning. The latter are *profane* ways of knowing. They pertain to profane reality, and as such they become impediments to a religious adherent as he or she becomes more perfectly oriented to ultimate reality.

Some traditions even understand the movement toward ultimate reality as a transformation of the adherent *into* ultimate reality. It is a union with God, a "becoming one" with the All, wherein the adherent sheds the trappings of profane reality. In these cases adherents are like a rocketship on its way to the sun. As it nears its destination, its instrumentation is disabled by the heat. If, for the purposes of this illustration, we think of the extreme temperature of the sun as a

> The reader is invited to direct his mind to a moment of deeply-felt religious experience. . . . Whoever cannot do this, whoever knows no such moments in his experience, is requested to read no farther.
>
> —*Rudolf Otto*[4]

higher reality (even though it is actually part of our physical reality), we may even picture our rocketship becoming "more real" as it moves away from earth's reality and is absorbed into the reality of the sun. Likewise in a religion: Enlightened adherents can become oriented to ultimate reality to such a degree that their experiences with this infinitely inscrutable mystery become part of the mystery.

In sum, the analysis of religions has an important limitation. While it advances our understanding of the "workings" of a religion—its symbols, its visions of realities, its inner-logic, and its change over time—it clarifies religions only from the perspective of profane reality. Yet religion, as orientation to ultimate reality, encompasses experiences that call for nonanalytic modes of knowing, and religious traditions, as symbolic systems for such orientation, touch on realities that are alien to analytical inquiry.

The Ethics of Analysis

Most of the world's religious adherents give little thought to the notion that their religion is one of many or that religion is a distinct aspect of their lives. These are the perspectives of secularized, pluralistic societies. Religious adherents in other societies see themselves as "getting on with life" and doing what is required, not "being religious" or "practicing religion"—let alone practicing *a* religion. They act in ways they understand to be right and necessary, in ways that are real and meaningful. Most "Hindus," for example, do not refer to their activities as "Hinduism," which is an outsider term. Instead they describe themselves as observing *dharma*, which is the *correct* ordering of the world and one's *proper* duty in society. Likewise, most "Buddhists" live according to *the* Four Noble Truths; most "Taoists" attempt to harmonize their lives with *the* Way; and most Jews, Christians, and Muslims describe themselves as obeying *the* will of *God*—not *a* god.

In each of these instances there lurks an implicit denial that one's own religious activities participate in any larger entity called "religion," at least in the sense that these activities are comparable to those in another religion. It would strike most Muslims as misguided, if not downright insidious, to suggest that the *Hajj*, the annual pilgrimage to Mecca, has the same religious function for a Muslim as a pilgrimage to the Western Wall does for a Jew. The one has been commanded by Allah, the other has not. Therefore, when students of religion use such terms as "religion" and "religions," they promote a view that is different, unwelcome, and often offensive or threatening to members of the religions they are analyzing.

The ethical dilemma posed by analysis comes into view more clearly when we acknowledge that "religion" and "religions" are the intellectual abstractions of academia. They are the scholarly tools of a secularized, and mostly Western, tradition of post-Enlightenment thought and, like other such abstractions, have never been fully accepted by those outside this narrow tradition. It is *we* (to put a face on these students of religion) who advance the notion that "religions" are comparable. It is *we* who hold that they share common elements and dynamic equivalents, and that Juda*ism* and Buddh*ism*, or Sunni and Shiite Islam, are, on some level, alike, equal, the same. In so doing, we, as students of religion, promote not simply a different way of knowing a religion, but an intellectual agenda. It is an ideology, even, as to how one should view the world, and it often stands in opposition to the very religions we analyze. Inasmuch as analysis does not endorse a particular religion as "necessary" or "true" or "the will of God," it relativizes that religion's vision of ultimate reality, and thereby undermines its validity in the eyes of its adherents.

This is true, moreover, even though the study of religion is not intended to be offensive to religious adherents. As we have seen, the analysis of religions requires the use of neutral categories such as "ultimate reality" and "symbol." As opposed to categories that might favor one religion over another, such as "messiah" or "sacrament," these are intended to be impartial in all religious contexts. Yet the neutrality of these categories is the heart of the problem. First, it is oxymoronic to speak of "*an* ultimate reality" or "ultimate realit*ies*." Either something is ultimate, and therefore unique, or it is not. And second, these are not the terms used by the adherents themselves when they give expression to what is most meaningful and real in their lives. Imagine addressing a Christian carrying a Bible or a Jew wearing a prayer shawl with the words, "I see you have a powerful symbol there. Are you on your way to orient yourself to an ultimate reality?" In the end, the neutrality that enables the analysis of religion is a virtue only for the outsider. For the insider, neutrality in the face of what is ultimate is "profane"—it is unreal or sinful, or both.

Not surprisingly, then, many religious adherents regard the study of religion as an intrusion into their lives. It can lead to painful "faith crises" among college students, "cognitive dissonance" in tribal communities, or culture wars that pit "religion" and "state" against one another and brand certain religions as "liberal" or "backward." To be sure, some people, both religious and nonreligious, hold that these faith crises and culture wars are inevitable, and even beneficial for society. But as we have seen, the study of religion has limitations. It can analyze religions only from an academic, "profane" worldview, and hence religious experience is always beyond its proper sphere of intellectual authority. Because of this limitation, and given the enormous power of persuasion that intellectualism has in Western culture, perhaps analysis should include some allowance for intellectual humility and respect for others. In the analysis of religions—those symbolic systems by which human beings establish ultimate meaning in their lives—academics need to adopt a professional ethic that recognizes the right of religious people simply to be left alone.

PART FOUR

COMPARISON AND EVALUATION

⪦chapter 14⪧

The Comparison of Religions

The comparison of religions explores meaningful similarities and differences between religions. Unlike the *evaluation* of religions (see chapter 16), it is undertaken for the purpose of learning more about religion and religions, whether or not one plans to use this knowledge to judge a religion's worth. Just as other fields of study have recognized the importance of a comparative subdiscipline—comparative government in political science, comparative anatomy in biology—so, too, the comparison of religions is an essential aspect of studying religion. As we noted earlier, familiarity with only one specimen of a thing, be it wine, business management models, or religions, courts intellectual myopia.

The starting point for comparison is the recognition that each religion is a coherent system and that its elements derive their meaning as parts of that system. Just as a word has no meaning when it is isolated from its proper system of language, the elements of a religion become opaque if we ignore their native context. When this happens, comparisons become arbitrary and biased, moving from neutral exploration to misunderstanding and condemnation.

For example, we might be tempted to compare the Christian Trinity of Father, Son, and Holy Spirit with the Hindu Trinity of Brahma, Vishnu, and Shiva. A simple listing of the characteristics of each Trinity would be easy enough. But if we overlook the fact that the former is central to the religion of most Christians, whereas the latter is an intellectual formulation of limited practical significance for most Hindus, this is like comparing the mathematical abilities of Albert Einstein and Mark Twain. The differences are marked and real, but not of any great value for understanding either figure.

> The Qur'an, it is said, is the Muslim Bible; the mosque is the Muslim church; the ulema are the Muslim clergy. All three statements are true, yet all three are seriously misleading.
>
> —*Bernard Lewis[1]*

Or again, we could compare the Jain promotion of nonviolence (*ahimsa*) with the sacrificial practices of ancient Judaism. In the one, priests go to great lengths to avoid harming any sentient creature, even gnats and slugs. In the other, priests butchered and roasted birds and beasts on the altar of God. Unless we take into account the larger systems of these religions, which include, respectively, a belief in *karma* and rebirth into nonhuman forms and a belief in God as Creator of the natural world and guardian of a chosen people, we not only venture into a pointless comparison, as in the previous example, but also risk coming to foregone conclusions based on *our* sensibilities about the sanctity of life. In neither case will we have addressed the subject on its own terms, on the basis of its own inner-logic.

Some comparisions of this sort are particularly tempting, as when the same symbol is used by more than one religion. Water, as we have noted, is one of these. Because so many religious traditions understand the profane world as "impure" and ultimate reality as "pure," orientation to the latter often takes the form of washing oneself "clean." This observation has encouraged a few scholars to speak of "universal symbols" or "patterns" of symbols.

Yet washing rituals can vary greatly between traditions. Hindu ablutions at sunrise are not the same as Christian baptism or a Shinto priest sprinkling an adherent with a wet evergreen sprig. It is also true that religions use water for ends other than purification. In Taoism and Zen Buddhism water orients adherents to a divine flow or Way, in agrarian religions water can connect adherents with the powers of life and regeneration, and in religions that rely on mythologies of sea gods and primal floods water orients adherents to such higher-order realities as chaos and evil. Thus, to the extent that there is no generic religion or universally held vision of ultimate reality, we must use considerable caution when speaking of common or universal symbols.

Fortunately, most of these pitfalls can be avoided if, in setting up a comparison, we take into account the larger systems of religions by identifying "dynamic equivalents." Instead of beginning with "obvious" similarities or "reasonable" points of comparison, which often have more to do with our worldviews than those of the religions in question, we need to locate elements that play "equivalent" roles within the "dynamics" of their respective religious systems. In this way, we can determine which comparisons are superficial and arbitrary, and which will lead us into a fuller understanding of the religions being compared. Sometimes elements that initially appear to have nothing in common emerge as informative dynamic equivalents. For instance, an Episcopalian walking through a stylized labyrinth or singing Taizé songs, an evangelical Protestant observing "quiet time," a Vaishnava Hindu chanting from the Vedas, and a Zen monk raking leaves are all "equivalent" symbolic acts within the dynamics of each religion. All are routine, "intentionless" activities that inhibit one's thoughts from focusing on profane reality. Each prepares the adherent's mind for interaction with ultimate reality, based on the manner in which each tradition envisions that reality.

This procedure of locating dynamic equivalents also allows the student of religion to postulate larger, comparative categories, such as "worship," "mysticism," and "initiation rite," *from within the religions themselves*, establishing a basis for comparing religions that is both "organic" and "reciprocal." In this way we avoid comparisons based on our own preconceptions and minimize the risk of understanding one religion in terms of another. Of course, in adopting this procedure, we must also reckon with another eventuality. If we confine our comparisons to elements that are dynamic equivalents, we will encounter instances in which no comparison is possible. We have no guarantee that every element in one religion will be matched by a dynamic equivalent in another. But this, too, is valuable information for the student of religion.

Finally, it needs to be said that the comparison of religions is more than just the intellectual pursuit of academics. Beyond informing the academic study of religion, it has a practical side, too. Amid the pluralism of American society, the comparison of religions enables us to "cope"—to fathom, to adjust to, and to enter into dialogue with those whose mores and lifestyles diverge from our own. Americans still struggle with racial and ethnic difference. Some attention to "comparative religious ethics" will prevent similar impasses over religious difference.

Furthermore, the comparison of religions can give people perspective on their place in their own religious tradition. Few religions are monolithic, and the diversity *within* religions becomes increasingly apparent as our world becomes more interconnected. Formerly separated by distance and time, different forms of the same religions now come into contact with each other

> The interfaith agenda, in all its complexity, is now America's agenda.
>
> —*Diana Eck*[2]

on a regular basis: first- and third-world evangelicals, high- and low-church Methodists, Orthodox and Conservative Jews, Italian and Irish Catholics, and Southern, Independent, and Free-Will Baptists. By knowing that each of these manifestations of a tradition differs from its cousins by virtue of different symbols and visions of realities, we may analyze and compare the various forms of a single denomination in the same way that one analyzes and compares Hinduism and Confucianism.

In fact, one need not venture outside of his or her own personal religious worldview to appreciate the value of comparing religions. Since all religions change over time, every religion has a history. Even persons who isolate themselves from every tradition but their own must, in some manner, reckon with past versions of that tradition. Present-day Mormonism is not what it was in the days of its founder, Joseph Smith, nor is early twentieth-century Catholicism the same as post–Vatican II Catholicism. If one sees oneself as standing in a particular tradition, as a modern representative of a historical faith (and most do), then one must adopt some identification vis-à-vis his or her forerunners.

This becomes especially urgent when a tradition defines itself with reference to a golden era—the first-century church, the first Buddhist *sangha*, the lifetime of Muhammad—or a sacred scripture. For example, the Bible has been scripture for ancient and

Religion mutates with Darwinian restlessness. Take a long enough view, and all talk of "established" or "traditional" faith becomes oxymoronic.

—*Toby Lester*[3]

modern Christians—as well as patristic, late antique, early medieval, high medieval, and Renaissance Christians—but not in the same way. Since the Bible is an ancient document, the oldest aspects of which are now several millennia old, using it to define the religion of the modern church requires a process of interpretation. Yet the question this interpretation must answer is not so much, How does the Bible speak to Christians (or Southern Baptists, or third-world evangelicals, or post–Vatican II Catholics) today?, for that has the potential of severing ties with the past. Rather, the question is, How *should* the Bible speak to Christians today, in light of how it *once* spoke to Christians in the past?[4] This type of interpretation, therefore, is really a matter of comparison. It compares past systems with present systems: how the Bible functioned as a symbol in the religious system of, say, medieval Christianity, as compared with the possibilities for it functioning as a symbol in the religious systems of Christianity today.

To shift to the language of theology, what we are speaking of here is "hermeneutics." This is the attempt, common to all religions, to keep a tradition viable and coherent by reappropriating past practices and beliefs. It is through hermeneutics that the example of Jesus, or the Buddha, or Muhammad, and the pronouncements of the Bible, or the *Pitakas*, or the Qur'an, remain relevant in today's world. Likewise, it is hermeneutics that determines whether a tradition will address this or that modern issue—stem-cell research, the "greenhouse" effect—or advance this or that modern cause—environmental justice, nuclear disarmament. Thus, understood as hermeneutics, the comparison of religions is far from an intellectual luxury. If a religion cannot justify the relevance of its tradition to each succeeding generation, it goes the way of "dead religions"—Mithraism, Gnosticism, and the religions of classical Greece and Rome and Egypt. It is swallowed up by a more viable tradition or becomes extinct.

ᔆchapter 15ᔆ

THE EVALUATION OF RELIGION

In these two final chapters we turn toward philosophical and political issues. In this chapter we ask whether there is really such a thing as religion; in the next we explore the possibilities for preferring one religion over another. To be sure, the question for the present chapter may strike the reader as odd, given our assumptions thus far. Nonetheless, it is a serious question, posed time and again by scholars in two distinct ways.

I

First, scholars have posed the question, Is there really such a thing as religion?, with the meaning, Is religion an irreducible entity in our world—a thing "unto itself"—or is it simply the product of some other entity, such as human psychology or sociology? Is religion, in other words, *sui generis* or derivative? The reader will remember that we raised this question back in chapter 2, only to leave it open until now.

In the last century and a half this question has been coupled with concerns for the *origin* and *truth* of religion. In the 1800s many scholars proposed that religion began as a misunderstanding on the part of early human beings. Either because early humans were confined to "primitive" modes of thought, resembling the imaginative thinking of children, or because they were simply prescientific in their approach to the physical world, they posited supernatural forces, spirits, and gods in an attempt to make sense of natural occurrences. Their interactions with these imagined entities, at the dawn of civilization, constituted that moment in history from which religion sprang and spread to the entire human race. With this line of scholarship we associate such figures as Ludwig Feuerbach, E. B. Tylor, James Frazer, Max Müller, and Lucien Lévy-Bruhl.

> We shall perhaps be disposed to conclude that the movement of the higher thought, so far as we can trace it, has on the whole been from magic through religion to science.
>
> —*Sir James Frazer[1]*

Others have proposed that religion did not begin at a certain point in history, but in the nonlogical, nonscientific aspects of human life. Scholars such as Sigmund Freud and Carl Jung proposed that religion is a by-product of the human psyche. Freud identified it as a neurosis, Jung as a part of normal psychological maturation. Still others have argued that religion arises from group interaction rather than individual psychology. Emile Durkheim, for example, argued that religion's true function was to establish authority in human societies, while Karl Marx denounced religion as a tool of political oppression.

In each of these theories religion is reduced to a more basic human reality; it is seen as "really" or "merely" an extension of something else. It is not, as most religious adherents of the world believe, orientation to ultimate reality, but orientation to what is human and mundane, including even misconceptions and vice. The common assumption of these theories, moreover, is that religion derives from the essential constitution of human beings, as individuals or as a collective. For our purposes in answering the question, Is there such a thing as "religion"?, we may therefore simplify these theories by proposing that there are really only two explanations for religion, a *biological* and a *theological* explanation.

The *biological* explanation, which sums up these theories,

> Scholarly interest in uncanny phenomena . . . should not be daunted by the possibility of their reality.
>
> —*Daniel Gold, summarizing the views of forklorist Andrew Lang*[2]

holds that there is something in the emotional and intellectual makeup of human beings—the human psyche—that creates a religious need in people, either individually or collectively. Since the psyche, from a scientific viewpoint, is a matter of electrochemical reactions and the firing of synapses, this explanation leads to the conclusion that human beings are *biologically conditioned* to be religious. One might want to argue, of course, that "nurture" also plays a role. But since some form of religion has been found in all cultures of the world, this consideration need not detain us here. The *theological* explanation, by contrast, holds that there exists a supernatural reality that calls to human beings, evoking certain responses that we call "religious."

To put the matter another way, there is either something *in* human beings naturally (biologically) that accounts for their religious behavior, or something supernatural that acts on them *from without*—or both. I see no fourth possibility. If this is correct, it becomes clear why the question, Is there such a thing as "religion"?, and its correlate, Is religion true?, resist definitive answers. To prove the biological explanation we would need to locate a "religion gene" in the human DNA, the removal of which would render people non-religious. To prove the theological explanation, we would have to provide evidence for higher-order realities or ultimate reality—that is, "proof of God."

> I
> f we destroy all life on the planet, religion will vanish too.
>
> —*Rodney Stark and William Bainbridge*[3]

Further, neither of these proofs, in themselves, is sufficient to disprove the competing theory. After all, God or ultimate reality could have planted a religion gene in the human DNA. Hence the only way to bring resolution to this matter is to "prove God," which seems unlikely, or *dis*prove God *and* locate the religion gene, which also seems unlikely. And perhaps this is no great surprise, given the limits of analysis we considered in chapter 12. As we noted there, it is the assertion of religious adherents that the experience of ultimate reality is, by virtue of its ultimacy, beyond the scope of analytical, scientific investigation.

II

In chapter 13 ("The Ethics of Analysis"), we made the case for "religion" being a scholarly abstraction. Accepting this as true, several students of religion have posed the question, Is there really such a thing as religion?, in a second manner: Is religion *only* an abstraction, or does it identify an actual entity in our world?

One might worry that the answer to this question is hopelessly entangled with the previous question of whether religion is *sui generis* or reducible to something more basic in the human psyche. As a matter of practicality many scholars in the last century have simply sidestepped that quandary, suggesting that we treat religion as *sui generis* unless it be proven otherwise. Major figures associated with this view include Raffaele Pettazzoni, Rudolf Otto, Gerardus van der Leeuw, Joachim Wach, and Mircea Eliade. Dissenting from this position, Jonathan Z. Smith has championed the view that until we can settle the question of religion's irreducibility, one should speak of "religion" only within academia, treating it as a convenient category of the scholar and no more. In line with this, some scholars prefer to speak of the study of religion*s*, or of a *particular* religious tradition. In their minds, the use of the generic "religion" seems to presuppose the reality of such an entity.

Yet our ability to answer this second question, Is religion *only* an abstraction?, need not depend on our ability to answer the first, Is religion an irreducible entity of our world?

> R
> eligion is solely the creation of the scholar's study. . . . Religion has no independent existence apart from the academy.
>
> —*Jonathan Z. Smith*[4]

Rather, the real impediment has been the inability of scholars to define religion.[5] When one cannot define a thing, it is naturally difficult to justify its use, and this has nothing to do with whether religion or religions are "truth." Science fiction, for example, which makes no truth-claims about the existence of its imagined worlds, is nonetheless a well-defined genre of literature.

Let us approach this question with the definition of religion used in this book, "orientation to ultimate reality." As we have seen, this orientation takes place through symbols, since ultimate reality is not directly accessible to the profane world. The use of symbols, however, is not unique to religion. At every stage of life, with the possible exception of infancy and senility, human beings act in ways that break the routine of life, imbuing it with meaning. They play with dolls and toy guns, they buy athletic shoes and memorize baseball statistics, all for the purpose of gaining access to "higher worlds" of meaning—be it the world of grown-ups, the world of fashion, or the world of larger-than-life sports heroes. All of these, moreover, are *symbolic* acts. They are a culture's designated "tools" for transcendence in particular cultural contexts. None has any necessary meaning apart from those contexts; none is "true" or "obvious" in any objective sense. Rather, they are effective, they "work," simply because a given culture says so.

Human beings, in other words, are symbolic creatures. They choose this or that thing according to the inner-logic of their cultures for the purpose of infusing their lives with meaning, thereby making life more important, more real, more worth living. From this perspective, religion may be understood as one aspect of the symbolic activity of human beings. When humans, in the course of using symbols, orient themselves not simply to higher worlds of meaning but to something ultimate, these symbols become "religious" symbols, and their activities become "religion." It is this ultimate point of reference that makes these activities distinct, and hence definable as a discrete category. In this sense, there really is such a thing as religion, and this will be true whether or not one can "prove the existence of God."

≼chapter 16≽

THE EVALUATION OF RELIGIONS

If we are correct in understanding human beings as symbolic creatures, then religion will always be with us—that is, as long as human beings seek to orient themselves to something ultimate. It is worth asking, then, whether one system or subsystem of religious practice is superior to another. Thus, rather than evaluating religion, as in the previous chapter, here we consider the possibilities, along with their implications, of favoring one religion over another. Is it possible to show that Christianity is better than Buddhism, that Methodist Christianity is better than Lutheran Christianity, or that one type of Methodism is superior to another?

PSEUDO-RELIGIONS

I think most would agree that if a religion is insincere, if its driving force is deception and personal gain and its principal characteristic is hypocrisy, it is bad. But this is not a religion by our definition. It is orientation to profane wealth, or power, or vice, not ultimate reality. It is a confidence game masquerading as a religion.

These "pseudo-religions" are, however, relatively rare in the world of religions, and we must not, on their account, judge entire traditions on the basis of a few individuals or conclude that money or power has no legitimate place in religion. The scandals of TV evangelists or the schemes of opportunistic gurus peddling the wisdom of the East invalidate neither Christianity nor Hinduism, nor even evangelical Christianity or tantric Yoga. Indeed, it is a premise of all religions that human beings are in need of some greater good, that their profane existences are filled with shortcomings. Hence, if our criterion for evaluating religions was the sincerity or perfection of its adherents, all religions would be self-condemning.

THE WORLD LOVES A WINNER

One approach to evaluating religions is the popular notion that the traditions with the most followers are the best. These are called "world religions" or "great traditions" as opposed to "native cults" or "sects." Crudely put, could nearly two billion Christians be wrong? In the nineteenth and early twentieth centuries, it was even popular to argue that human history selects the best religious systems: Religions that adapt and thrive are good; those that dwindle and die are bad.

Yet this approach assumes a model of progress in history that is difficult to defend, and everyday experiences tell us that "the best" does not always triumph, unless we define "best" in a circular manner as "successful." Video specialists still regard the defunct BETA format as technically superior to VHS, and blind taste tests indicate that a majority of Americans think Pepsi tastes better than Coke. So: Could 1.9 billion Christians be wrong? Possibly yes, just as 1.2 billion Muslims or 1.2 billion communist Chinese might also be wrong. And conversely, Judaism, Zoroastrianism, and the Mandaean religion are no less right for having only 14.4 million, 2.5 million, and 38,000 adherents, respectively.

THE "ESSENCE" OF RELIGIONS

A second approach is to pronounce *all* religions good and leave the choice among them to personal preference. Because all religions are "essentially the same," so the argument goes, one is as good as another, if practiced sincerely. There are many paths to the One Truth; the Divine Light shines in everyone. In its most pedestrian form in the West, this view is held by people who know little about religions and is more an expression of political correctness or disinterest than serious reflection. An exception to this, certainly, are the views of religious theorists such as Mircea Eliade or Joseph Campbell. These scholars emphasize the generic nature and organic unity of religious phenomena. Yet their conclusions

> Eliade's theory is in its own way philosophical and speculative. . . . It seems to me that we have a problem where a theory in effect is an expression of a worldview, which is then brought to bear upon worldviews.
>
> —*Ninian Smart[1]*

rest on particular schools of thought, such as humanism, phenomenology, and Jungian psychology, and are valid only insofar as one chooses to embrace these ideologies.

Another exception is religious adherents who engage in ecumenical and interfaith dialogues. Their belief in the essential unity of all "people of faith" has promoted understanding and mutual respect between traditions and resulted in the melding of some religious traditions with others: Roman Catholicism with Lutheranism, or Christianity with Buddhism. But this type of collegial evaluation of another tradition is not always possible, as when "radical" or "fundamentalist" traditions resist pluralistic solutions. Thus, while ecumenical and interfaith movements can sometimes lead to peaceful coexistence with one's neighbors, they do not provide an adequate basis for evaluation, which is our focus here.

CREATING NEW RELIGIONS

On the other hand, when pluralistic theologies are pursued to their logical limits, the result is not ecumenism or interfaith movements, but new religions altogether. Here evaluation becomes a process of selecting out superior elements from the entire spectrum of religious traditions rather than choosing from among traditions already in existence. An example of this in the modern world is the Baha'i religion; others include New Age religions, neo-paganism, and various traditions of spirituality such as "womanist spirituality."

In contrast to the nineteenth-century claim that certain religions improved over time through humanity's moral evolution, these religions are deliberate attempts to incorporate into a single tradition the very best of all religions. The designers of these new traditions avail themselves of religious practices from across the globe and throughout the ages. In the United States, goddess worship, gnosticism, Asian spirituality, tribal wisdom, and witchcraft have become popular resources for creating new religions. But apart from questioning the viability and artificiality of these new religions, the more important question for us concerns criteria: What constitutes "superior elements"? Are there objective criteria for creating and promoting certain religions in this way?

> New Age is . . . a manifestation *par excellence* of postmodern consumer society, the members of which use, recycle, combine and adapt existing religious ideas and practices as they see fit.
>
> —*Wouter Hanegraaff*[2]

A COMMON CRITERION?

First, let us consider whether we can establish a criterion for evaluating religions that is common to all religions. It has been popular since the publication of William James's *Varieties of Religious Experience* to suggest that religions be evaluated "by their fruits."[3] That is, the value of a religion should be determined by the benefits it brings to human society, not by its doctrines or ideals. The problem with this proposal is twofold. First, any "benefit" one names, be it social justice or the dissemination of love or reason, will be emphasized in one tradition more than another, and absent altogether from others. How it can serve as a "common" criterion, therefore, is unclear, for through the process of selecting a particular benefit we will already have favored some religions over others.

Second, the notion that a particular benefit is understood in the same way by two or more traditions is an illusion. Take love as an example. Are we speaking of Hindu devotional love (*bhakti*), Jewish covenantal love (*hesed*), Buddhist compassion (*karuna*), Taoist nonaggression (*wu-wei*), Confucian filial piety (*hsiao*), or Christian sac-

> **R**eligions are not all the same, but many are humanly acceptable.
>
> —*Willard Oxtoby[4]*

rificial love (*agape*)? And even if we could establish, say, Hindu devotional love as our standard, would it be the type accorded to Shiva, or Parvati, or Vishnu? If to Vishnu, then in his incarnation as Krishna? And if so, would this be a mother's devotion to Krishna the child, a teenager's romantic love for Krishna the youthful cowherd, or the mystic's love for Hare Krishna?

> **I**f the Chinese "believe" in spirits in anything like the way my Long Island community believed in papal authority, or even the way Christian colleagues believe in a central doctrine like the divinity of Christ, then the statement that the Chinese believe in ancestral spirits is, at best, a very vague generalization that ignores everything interesting.
>
> —*Catherine Bell[5]*

Worse still, what passes as "reason" in Christianity is seen by some religions as intellectual imperialism, and what Hindu *dharma* defines as "social justice" strikes many as social oppression. One can even find these disparities within a single tradition: Well-being to the laity can be wasteful excess to an ascetic order of holy men, and one person's theological openness is another's heresy.

Be that as it may, one might respond, is it therefore impossible to define common ground between at least *some* religions, thereby establishing *some* common criterion for evaluation? After all, the evaluation of religions implies that some religions will fare better than others; so maybe finding an agreement on norms among a majority or plurality of religions should be our target, rather than unanimity or consensus. Furthermore, have not certain visionary theologians located just such common ground between their traditions and those of others; and as theologians, should they not be given special credence as leading spokespersons for their traditions?

As appealing as this suggestion might sound, it is no more than a variant of the notion that the most popular religions are the best, which we considered earlier. Even if a majority of the world's adherents agree on certain religious norms, this does not establish their superiority in any objective way—no more than the popularity of xenophobia establishes its superiority. It is simply rule by the majority.

Beyond this we must understand the role of "theology" in "religion." Religion is orientation to ultimate reality; theology is an attempt to reflect on, articulate, and systematize that orientation. While theologians can usually articulate their traditions more persuasively than nontheological adherents, especially to outsiders, their role in a religion should not be overstated. Viewed strictly as a religious activity—as a means of orientation—"doing theology" or "theologizing" is only one of the many symbolic activities of a given religion. Thus, even when theologians of the stature of Mahatma Gandhi, Paul Tillich, Eli Wiesel, Hans Küng, or the Dalai Lama have seen their way clear to reconciling two or more traditions *theologically*, it is not at all evident just how much common ground they have established or for whom, for in their role as theologians they constitute only a small aspect of their respective traditions. From the perspective of fellow insiders, moreover, theologians who work to establish common criteria with other traditions are often viewed as heterodox or as hybrid creatures, every bit as problematic as students of religion. Part analyst, by virtue of their interest in the comparison of religions, and part adherent, by virtue of their orientation to ultimate reality, they stand at the margins of their own religions, looking out from the inside and in from the outside.

AN INDEPENDENT CRITERION?

If we are unable to establish a common criterion for evaluating religions, perhaps we can do without one. Maybe we need to adopt a criterion that is independent of religious traditions altogether, and in that way "neutral." Basic human goods such as love, justice, and reason once again suggest themselves. The problem is that none of these values is neutral in an absolute sense. While they may be independent of a given religion, all of them stem from *some* worldview—*some* understanding of what is real and has meaning. Even the seemingly innocuous position that religions should all respect one another falls short, for implicit in this "should" is a value system. None of these criteria is more correct than the others unless we agree beforehand on the superiority of its underlying worldview.

Furthermore, religions are themselves systems whose point of reference is something superior (ultimate). In evaluating a religion in this manner one is thus obligated to pass judgment on that religion's vision of ultimate reality—but is this possible? If the basis of our criterion is anything less than something ultimate, it will fare poorly against the claims of a given religion, to the extent that it is "less real" and "less meaningful." Even such ideals as mutual respect and religious freedom are questionable or wrong in the face of *divine* inspiration.

The only way around this quagmire is to discredit a religion's vision of ultimate reality by disproving it, or to claim something ultimate as the basis of our own worldview. As we have suggested, however, it is impractical to "disprove God." Yet if we choose the latter path, we have, by our definition, espoused a religion. In this instance we are doing nothing more than evaluating one religion in terms of another, as when a Buddhist judges Islam on the basis of Buddhist ideals.

"CHURCH AND STATE" (RELIGION AND GOVERNMENT)

In a religiously pluralistic society like the United States, the inability to establish an independent criterion for evaluating religions can create enormous problems. How should Christians treat the Muslims or Buddhists down the street? How much community can exist between partisans oriented to competing visions of ultimate reality? Who is to say that Southern Baptists should not target Roman Catholics and Jews for conversion? Maybe they are correct; and if not, can one demonstrate their incorrectness apart from espousing an equally partisan point of view?

It is also true that just as some religious adherents emphasize tolerance, others view *in*tolerance as a means of orientation to ultimate reality. In these instances exclusivity has become a symbol. Thus, when certain Islamist groups in the United States declare a holy struggle (*jihad*) against this country, it is not a contradiction of religion, or "true religion," or even their own religious tradition. It is only a contradiction of *other* peoples' religious traditions and views of life. What we condemn as "suicide bombings" others revere as "sacred explosions." God (ultimate reality) has commanded these things.

Just as religions can give adherents the requisite inner strength to resist in the face of persecution, exile, and death, they also can promote these things. So also with retaliation, untouchability, and the subordination of women. These things are all "good," "necessary," and "holy" in some religious traditions. Is society, in these cases, justified in defining—and legislating—morality? On what basis and to what extent?

If society *is* justified, then we are confronted with an even larger problem: Are *various* societies justified in defining morality? How will these societies come to terms with one another? As the world community becomes more integrated, the problems of religious pluralism that face individual societies will become international issues. Rather than asking, How should Christians treat the Muslims or Buddhists down the street?, the question will be, How should a Muslim nation treat its Buddhist, pluralistic, and secular neighbors?

The true complexity of this problem becomes clear when we reflect on our definition of religion. Religion is orientation to ultimate reality. This orientation necessitates the use of "symbols," understood as tools for achieving this orientation. Each religious tradition, in turn, provides a coherent system of symbols, held together by that religion's inner-logic. When religious traditions come into contact with one another, either in a pluralistic society or a pluralistic world, it is primarily on the basis of these symbols that their respective adherents take offense: I do not like your treatment of women, you do not like my zeal for evangelizing your young people; you cannot tolerate my caste system, I cannot abide your materialism. I deem certain of your symbols inappropriate, you feel the same about mine.

But this is only the symptom, not the basis of the problem. Although symbols are the point of contact between religions, and therefore the cause of friction, the underlying problem is the religions' respective visions of ultimate reality, for these dictate what is and what is not appropriate as a symbol. Once a vision of ultimate reality is in place, using the designated symbols is simply the way things need to be done. These symbols are nonnegotiable unless an adherent is willing to reenvision ultimate reality. This, however, is a tall order, not only because visions of ultimate reality often depend on profound religious experiences, but also because religious adherents rarely understand their traditions as systems of symbols and visions of profane, ultimate, and higher-order realities. As we have noted, most adherents do not even see themselves as "participating in a religious tradition," but as living life in the proper way. To them the possibility of "another" ultimate reality, let alone "other" or "multiple" ultimate realities, is a non sequitur.

> The challenge for contemporary people is how to live within some system of comprehensive evaluation (as found in a religion . . .) and how to respond in a mutually life-enhancing way with people committed to another system of evaluation.
>
> —*Frederick Streng*[6]

Something as grand as re-envisioning ultimate reality is, in any case, the business of prophets and reformers, not the average adherent or theologian. Furthermore, in the usual course of things, the more dramatic an innovation, the less credible it appears to adherents. This is why a détente between religions worked out by visionary theologians often resonates so poorly with practitioners. Nor should we assume that prophets and reformers always seek religious détente. They do not. They are first and foremost beholden to their experiences with ultimate reality, which, if history is a gauge, are more likely to be out of step than in step with pluralism and ecumenism.

SOLUTIONS

For pluralistic societies like the United States, the solution can only be a practical one. Lacking a common or neutral ground for evaluating religions, these societies must take the high ground. This is because being a religious adherent is never identical with being a citizen, unless one's religion is the state religion. When orientation to ultimate reality and the security of the state are not the same, there will come times when religious citizens will choose orientation to ultimate reality over patriotism. Since God is not an American, every Christian cannot always be a good American, just as every Jew and every Muslim cannot.

Indeed, lacking a common or neutral criterion by which they can evaluate the various religious traditions, citizens will choose a religion and evaluate the religions of others from an entirely partisan point of view. And I see nothing wrong with this. I see nothing wrong with this because I see no alternative. All religious

> **R**eligions are in effect independent centers of power.... A religion speaks to its members in a voice different from that of the state, and when the voice moves the faithful to action, a religion may act as a counterweight to the authority of the state.
>
> —*Stephen Carter*[7]

adherents, which encompasses most of humanity, will, to the extent that they are religious, be partisans. It is quite proper for them to condemn religious terrorism as evil, despite others' views that it is the work of saints, or to praise the Southern Baptists for their determination to convert Roman Catholics. It is also their prerogative to weigh in on world trade, abortion rights, the spread of capitalism, definitions of purity, standards of religious dress, and so on.

In other words, despite what readers may have been led to believe by the earlier discussion, I am not an advocate of religious relativism. As we have seen, human beings are religious by their very nature—biologically hardwired, divinely predestined, or both. It is their destiny in life to find an ultimate point of reference and, because it is ultimate, to orient themselves to it above all else. They cannot do otherwise.

> **I**t belongs to a religion to claim to be the true religion.
>
> —*Schubert Ogden*[8]

Because this partisan and potentially disruptive nature of religions argues against complete religious freedom in societies, religious pluralism will always be limited by a society's need to survive. This can be done through a consensus of the citizenry as to what is good, just, and wholesome, or through the dogma that the state itself is an essential good. Either way, a society must qualify the claim of its religious adherents that they are oriented to something infinitely superior to all else. Even pluralistic societies must be partisan and intolerant at some level. They must blunt the divisive nature of religion by (1) promoting a "civil religion"; (2) encouraging secularism, agnosticism, or atheism; or (3) pursuing a combination of these alternatives.

> **T**errorist fundamentalists from the Islamic world . . . have it exactly right when they oppose "the West," and especially America, for the invention of religious freedom.
>
> —*Martin Marty*[9]

Of course, a society need not be pluralistic, but this only throws the problem of pluralism onto an international venue. If some nations are dominated by a single religion, all nations will need to address the instability created by competing forms of religious partisanship, establishing limits to partisanship in matters that threaten shared interests. These matters will include more than just "religious concerns," narrowly defined. They will bear on global trade, ecology, world health, family planning, social justice, women's rights, nationalism, ethnicity, the spread of capitalism, and the spread of democracy. They will encompass anything that can be used as a symbol—anything valued or despised by virtue of one's orientation to ultimate reality—which is potentially *everything*.

THE BOTANIST AND THE GARDENER

By way of conclusion I offer a comparison between the student of religion and the religious adherent, on the one hand, and the botanist and the gardener, on the other. Botanists are those who study plants. It is not their place to endorse one plant over another, but to examine the members of the plant world, identify their peculiarities, and, ideally, develop a "critical appreciation" for all of them. Botanists, *as botanists*, do not assign "goodness" or "badness" to plants. They use the term "weed" only in descriptions of what others think, as in, "this species is considered a weed by most gardeners." Likewise, adjectives such as "invasive," "rangy," or "woody" will be used descriptively, not judgmentally. In their approach, these "students of flora" are like students of religion.

Gardeners, by contrast, are like adherents of religions. They exercise choice, judging some plants good or superior, and others bad or inferior. Since there is no common or independent criterion for making such evaluations, they, like religious adherents, are necessarily partisans. They love some plants and hate others. The ones they love can be poisonous, prickly, or "extremist" plants, such as "extremely aggressive" forms of bamboo. If they must, gardeners will protect those they love against those they despise. They will call the latter "smelly," "sticky," "ugly," or "weedy," and pull them out by the roots or spray them with herbicide. In this regard, the gardener, like the religious adherent, is neither neutral nor "just."

At the risk of extending this comparison beyond its usefulness, let me also suggest four kindred analogies. First, just as appraising plants solely on the basis of abundance or hardiness is a procedure of dubious worth, so also (as we maintained earlier) is the evaluation of religions in terms of their size or success. Wildflowers are not, in any absolute sense, "better" than orchids.

Second, just as botanists, through personal conviction, sometimes step beyond their neutral, academic roles and become impassioned preservationists, we find a similar advocacy for religious pluralism among students of religion. Recent examples of such students-of-religion-turned-advocates include Ninian Smart, Huston Smith, and Diana Eck.

Third, theologians compare favorably to "professional gardeners." As we have seen, they fall somewhere between students of religion and nontheological religious adherents. As such they often have some of the botanist's critical appreciation for a variety of plants as well as a partisan interest in their own gardens.

Fourth, it also seems apt to think of societies as "corporate growers." Societies that sponsor a single religion will specialize in nurturing it to the exclusion of others and will insist on standards of uniformity and purity. Those that support religious pluralism will work to preserve balance and diversity among the species, taking measures against any particular species that threatens to engulf the garden.

Finally, let us reflect on the notion that neutrality is the virtue of the botanist, while partisanship is the prerogative of the gardener. In analyzing religions, it is critical that we maintain this distinction between student and adherent, between analysis and religious participation. While students of religion can be adherents, too, they cannot be students and adherents simultaneously. As a student engaged in the analysis of religions, I cannot give preference to one religion over another; as a Christian, I can and must. In this sense I cannot be a "Christian student of religion." Even so, in Western countries at least, religious adherents will need the services of students of religion if they wish to participate in public discourse on religion. Just as the informed gardener depends on the botanist's nonpartisan analysis of plants, so also an orderly consideration of religions will depend on the nonpartisan analysis of religions. As centuries of partisan analysis and comparison have taught us, it benefits no one when students of religion mix analysis with religious loyalties, favoring one religion over others.

CONCLUSION

There is plenty of religion in modern American life—as well as in other cultures around the world and throughout the annals of human civilization. What has been lacking in modern America is a tradition of talking about religion in a way that promotes thoughtful analysis. This book has attempted to provide some ground rules for that undertaking. Here is a summary of what I consider to be its main contributions.

First, this book provides a definition of religion that can be accepted by both adherents and nonadherents. Unlike many other definitions, "orientation to ultimate reality" does not require one to affirm or deny the truth of one's own religion, or the truth of religion per se, in order to use it. As we have argued, the question of whether ultimate reality exists cannot be answered from an analytical perspective. Its affirmation or denial, therefore, cannot be a prerequisite for public discourse. So, too, with the other terms integral to our approach. Symbol, inner-logic, profane reality, and higher-order reality are also respectful of both religious and nonreligious sensitivities. Thus, in adopting this definition and what it implies, religious people need not become methodological atheists or agnostics to talk about religion publicly, and nonreligious people can take part in the discussion as something more than critics or disruptive outsiders.

Second, in keeping with this neutral approach, this book promotes the study of religion, but not religion itself. Because there is no agreement among the people of the world as to which religion is best, and because we hold different views on the benefits and drawbacks of each others' religions, and of religion per se, more religious commitment in our society or around the world—more orientation to ultimate reality—is not clearly a good thing. Naturally, as a religious adherent myself, I can have my own views on this subject, and I expect that readers will have their own views. But in the interest of sponsoring public discourse, we must be very clear on this one point: The study of religion must be distinct from the practice and promotion of religion. It is unfortunate for everyone involved when this distinction is blurred

> For many scholars in the field, the study of religion is a religious act.
>
> —*Marsha Hewitt*[1]

by those who should know better: theologians, politicians, religious activists, and, yes, academics.

Finally, this book has been intent on demonstrating that one *can* make sense of religion analytically, and that religion *is* more than just a personal matter, understood only by insiders. In contrast to the practice of religion or the appreciation of religion, the *study* of religion is not an introspective, spiritual undertaking, nor must its results be expressed in mystical or vague theological language. Terms like ultimate reality, inner-logic, and symbol can have precise meanings; and while the study of religion may lack the precision of mathematics or physics—a precision also lacking in the social sciences—it can nonetheless lead to clear, exacting conclusions.

In claiming this, moreover, I do not mean to deny that religion is many things to many people or that it can be approached in many different ways. Religion is like the ocean. It is a vast and complex system with its own share of mystery and paradox. No one knows it fully; no one comprehends it fully. Many are fascinated by it, inspired by it, and overwhelmed by it. And some even feel awe in its presence. Yet none of this should keep us from studying religion, just as none of it prevents us from studying the ocean. If religion is like the ocean, the analysis of religion is like oceanography.

POSTSCRIPT: SCIENCE AND RELIGIONS

In chapter 16 we considered the possibility of evaluating religions by means of a criterion that is independent of any particular religious tradition. One option we did not consider is whether science can provide such a criterion. The purpose of this postscript is to address that question and, more generally, to offer some perspective on the relation between science, religion, and religions.

Science, by which I mean both the scientific method and the data it produces, has become the centerpiece of Western intellectualism. It was even popular in the last century to argue that science had discredited religion as a legitimate human activity and would eventually replace theology as a guide for human thought and action. Worldwide, however, religion was never in danger of extinction. Even in the United States, where the advancement of science is promoted as a national priority, we have seen a growing fascination with religion since the 1960s—a period that has witnessed some of science's greatest accomplishments.

> No, our science is no illusion. But an illusion it would be to suppose that what science cannot give us we can get elsewhere.
>
> —*Sigmund Freud*[1]

That science did not succeed in disproving *religion* is not surprising, given our discussion in chapter 15. Yet the question before us now is whether science can nonetheless provide an independent criterion for evaluating *religions*. Since science establishes "facts" about the "truth" of things, can it not provide a neutral means of ranking or otherwise assessing the worth of religious traditions? The short answer to this question is no. Because Western civilization is so enamored with science, however, this is difficult for most people in the West to understand.

Let us take an example. The telling of myths is a symbolic act used by most, if not all, religions. It can be a powerful tool for orienting people to ultimate reality. But myths contain a great deal that is nonfactual and historically inaccurate. This is not a new observation, of course; even ancient Greeks were skeptical about the historical and logical consistency of their myths. It might seem appropriate, then, to evaluate religions on the basis of their reliance on mythology. Those that are more firmly entrenched in this nonfactual means of orientation would be judged inferior; those less entrenched, superior. If this approach were viable, then science would indeed provide an apt means for evaluating religions.

The problem with science is the same as the problem with all "independent criteria." As we determined in chapter 16, each of these depends on the acceptance of a specific view of the world. Unless its particular worldview can be established as superior, neither science nor any other standard can serve as an unbiased criterion for the evaluation of religions. It will always be a criterion from some particular viewpoint, having validity only from that perspective.

But, one might ask, is not factual information always superior to nonfactual information? And does it not follow that religions making greater use of mythology are, at least in *that* respect, inferior to others? And does it not follow from this that science offers the essential criterion for evaluating religions in this way?

While it is correct that the scientific method can determine which religious symbols, including myths, are scientifically and historically true, it is not correct that this necessarily has any relevance for the evaluation of religions. Symbols, as we have defined them, are the means or "tools" that religious people use for orientation to ultimate reality. In what way can we speak of them as "true" or "false"? Is it meaningful to say that a hammer or a screwdriver is true or false? Rather, as with any tool, the principal question for a symbol is whether or not it "works." That is, is it an appropriate way to orient oneself to ultimate reality?

> **R**eligious truth, and even some scientific truth, is greater than the power of the human mind to comprehend. . . . This creates the necessity for myth. . . . Even science needs rhetoric and resorts to myth-making.
>
> —*George A. Kennedy*[2]

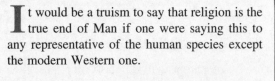

> **I**t would be a truism to say that religion is the true end of Man if one were saying this to any representative of the human species except the modern Western one.
>
> —*Arnold Toynbee*[3]

As we have seen, a symbol's appropriateness is determined solely by a religion's "inner-logic," which depends, in turn, on its vision of ultimate reality. For this reason, the focus of our inquiry must shift from symbols to a religion's inner-logic and vision of ultimate reality. Instead of asking whether science can evaluate a religion on the basis of its symbols (such as myths), we must ask if science can evaluate a religion by gauging the veracity of its inner-logic or vision of ultimate reality. Then we must ask if this is decisive in itself, and whether it has any bearing on the appropriateness of symbols.

With this change of focus, however, it also becomes necessary to remember that science has reference only to the reality of the material universe—a re-

> I f religion is as natural and science is as unnatural as I have argued, science poses no significant challenge to religion. Indeed, if my analysis is correct, it is the preservation of science that should concern us—its current prominence notwithstanding.
>
> —*Robert McCauley[4]*

ality that most religions associate with "profane reality." By contrast, the symbols of a religion, as well as its inner-logic and vision of ultimate reality, have reference to something ultimate. For religious adherents, then, a scientific point of reference can seem less meaningful, less true, less "real"—in every way less desirable—than an orientation to life made possible through religious symbols. On this reckoning it becomes difficult for science to provide a compelling criterion for the evaluation of religions, even when a religion's inner-logic and vision of ultimate reality have been determined to be *non*factual, *non*historical, and *non*scientific, or even *counter*factual, *un*historical, and scientifically *false.*

For example, beginning with the Enlightenment, religious adherents in the West have experienced what has been called a "crisis of faith." Even so, the result of this has not been a uniform rejection of Christianity, the West's dominant religious tradition, in favor of other religions or no religion at all. In light of scientific discoveries, some, it is true, "lose" their religious tradition or become agnostic toward it. Many more, however, question the reliability or the relevance of the scientific data that challenge their religion. And many others come to the conclusion that only certain symbols of their religion, like the biblical account of Creation, the doctrine of the resurrection, or the supremacy of a male priesthood, have lost their appropriateness, and simply turn to other Christian symbols for orientation to God.

In view of these considerations, it cannot be said that science offers a decisive criterion for the evaluation of religions. It can serve as a criterion only for those who envision ultimate reality as beholden, in some important way, to the material world and the standards of science. For this reason science is partisan, and no more definitive than the worldview of a particular religious tradition.

To gain a better sense of why people in the West often assume that science has the ability to evaluate religions, we need to recognize that Western intellectualism has been blinkered by a confusion between scientific "fact," on the one side, and "truth," on the other. In Western public discourse it is usually taken for granted that fact *is* truth, or that facts necessarily undergird truth. Yet here Western public discourse actually misrepresents its own underlying cultural sentiment.

Despite its exaggerated focus on the material world, even Western culture recognizes that not every truth is quantifiable as a scientific fact. Quite the contrary. Western civilization has always valued "artistic truth," as expressed in the fine arts, literature, and the performing arts. It also pays homage to the truth inherent in freedom, equality, love, and friendship, none of which is quantifiable in a way that can account for its importance to our culture. Western consumers, furthermore, regularly disregard the material facts of consumer products. People in the West do not buy cars, entertainment, or athletic shoes primarily on the basis of facts or by using the scientific method. Other things enter in, such as impulse, fashion, and sex appeal. In the parlance of American advertising, an industry that has shaped Western culture as much as anything has in the last half-century, "*image* is everything." Image, in other words, while it may have little to do with scientific fact, is "truth"—indeed, image becomes *truer* than fact.

My point here, simply, is that in the West, as elsewhere, truth is not confined to reason or to data. Rather, it is determined by meaning. This is why even scientists in the West—rational, objective men and women of science—are routinely drawn to the "truth" of music, philosophy, metaphysics, and religions.

> The heart has its reasons of which reason knows nothing: we know this in countless ways.
>
> —*Blaise Pascal*[5]

Because truth is dependent on meaning, not reason or data, Western culture also recognizes different levels of truth. Some facts are, frankly, more important than others. No biography of Winston Churchill records the number of pots of tea he consumed in his lifetime. Although this is a quantifiable fact, it is less meaningful, and therefore belongs to a "lesser order of truth," than many other facts of his life. Beyond this, facts do not necessarily constitute even the most important level of truth in the West. On a regular basis, Westerners will favor truth that rests on no facts over truth that rests on facts. Most Westerners, for example, regard telephone books as belonging to a "lesser order of truth" than great works of fiction, even though the former are chock full of facts, while the latter are deliberately nonfactual.

Thus, despite the tenor of its public discourse—its lip service to the superiority of science—Western culture has never regarded science as king. Its general public and its intellectuals alike have roundly rejected the notion that the world should be interpreted entirely or primarily through what Einstein once praised as the "grim objectivity" that results from scientific training.[6]

It might be helpful at this point to remind ourselves that the various disciplines of science are, to a large extent, symbolic systems. On that score science and religion have more in common than most Westerners realize. As an activity, science can be described as a way in which people orient themselves and others to the material world, or "orientation to material reality." The different fields of science, in turn, provide tools for this orientation. Some of these tools are symbolic, such as mathematical formulas and computer-generated models of molecular interaction. These orient scientists to the reality of the material world through nonmaterial strategies and procedures, just as religious symbols orient religious adherents to ultimate reality through nonultimate, profane means.

Other tools of science, of course, are not symbolic: the thermometer, the x-ray machine, the seismograph. Being part of physical reality themselves, these tools interact directly, not symbolically, with physical reality. Even these tools, however, depend on the symbolic tools of science, for the data they retrieve or the reaction they elicit requires theoretical, and therefore symbolic, interpretation. Otherwise, scientists could not properly orient themselves to the physical reality they were examining. So just as religions enable people to coordinate profane and ultimate reality, the sciences, as symbolic systems, enable people to coordinate the inner landscape of human intelligence with the external world of physical reality.

It might be objected here that, unlike profane and ultimate realities, the workings of the human mind do not really constitute a reality distinct from the physical world. They are themselves a part of the physical world, being so many electrochemical reactions in an enormously complex, carbon-based microchip. But this is not an established fact, nor even a widely held theory. Indeed, the vast majority of people in the world, including prominent scientists, reject a purely mechanical, materialist understanding of human mental processes because it does not seem to account for all the data. Except in the opinion of doctrinaire materialists, science does not yield a satisfactory explanation for common human experiences such as goodness, evil, love, or even something as quantifiable as time. Instead, the vast majority of humanity prefers to account for these things by postulating the existence of a nonmaterial ("spiritual") self or soul.

What emerges from these considerations is the necessity to admit that there are multiple, "parallel" symbolic systems in the world, each of which enables human beings to orient themselves to some aspect, or "reality," of the world, but none of which has a clear monopoly on meaning or truth. Perhaps this is because people themselves are diverse. Some tend more toward mathematics, some more toward

> Science acknowledges no free will in the usual sense at all. And yet, I believe I have free will. I sense it very strongly; I think almost every other individual does.
>
> —*Charles Townes*[7]

poetry, some more toward Hinduism. Until one of these symbolic systems can offer a convincing, unified theory of *all* reality or realities, truth will remain both fragmented *and plural*. This means, for example, that Christians who await the second coming of Christ, Buddhists who attain a sense of mindfulness, and cosmologists who hold to the Big Bang theory will orient themselves to the reality of time in different ways. It also means that we must continue to recognize that the division of humanity into castes and outcastes can be every bit as true and meaningful for a Hindu as a Westerner's understanding of genetic identities based on DNA analysis—every bit as true and meaningful, if not more so.

This is what is called "pluralism," and we see here that it does not encompass simply differences in cultural perspectives, but, more broadly, the differences in orientation between symbolic systems. Western academics have known this for quite some time, and have, as a consequence, founded universities. These institutions provide intellectual environments in which the different symbolic systems known as "scholarly disciplines" can "talk to one another." Some-

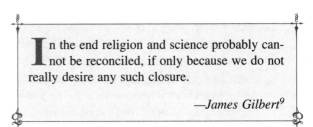

> Works of art, like "religious data," have a mode of being that is peculiar to themselves; *they exist on their own plane of reference*, in their particular universe. The fact that this universe is not the physical universe of immediate experience does not imply their non-reality.
>
> —*Mircea Eliade*[8]

times members of one discipline, say, education, will even speak of another discipline, say, classical studies, as having a different disciplinary "culture."

In many ways, however, the university has failed. Some disciplines seem not to communicate with others in any meaningful way. The result is that the integration of the disciplines has never penetrated much beyond the general liberal arts education. While undergraduates may study a number of disciplines, from social anthropology to physics, whatever interdisciplinary dialogue this generates effectively

> In the end religion and science probably cannot be reconciled, if only because we do not really desire any such closure.
>
> —*James Gilbert*[9]

ends at the graduate level, where specialization is required.

For our present discussion we need only point out that even in the environment of the university, doctors of science have little truck with doctors of theology. If we then take into account that there are also non-Western universities, populated by doctors of non-Western sciences and non-Western theologies—for example, long-standing Buddhist and Muslim universities—then the vision of the university as a place of meaningful dialogue begins to unravel even further. But let us keep our inquiry limited to the relation between *Western* science and religions.

The question I have been leading up to is this: We have argued that religions and Western science offer "parallel" symbolic systems of orientation. Let us now also grant, for the sake of argument, that dialogue between them is at least possible. Is it also the case that dialogue between science and religions is *necessary*?

From the perspective of a given religious tradition, it would appear that it may not be. As long as a religion understands scientific analysis and scientific

> I t's probably good for both those who sub-scribe to a secular scientific worldview and for theists to have one another around to remind themselves that, for all they know, the world might be a very different place than they imagine.
>
> —*Daniel Garber*[10]

data to be part of profane reality, science will be more or less irrelevant to the degree that it is less real than ultimate reality. As long as a religion recognizes a reality higher than the material world, it will see science as proffering only second-tier truths. It is so much *maya* (illusion), as a Hindu or Buddhist might put it.

Beyond this, however, even when religions accord a substantial degree of importance and reality to the truths of Western science, they may not see dialogue as necessary. This is because "parallel" truths do not have to be competing or interacting truths. Artistic truth and scientific truth, for instance, have long existed side-by-side in our culture without any significant dialogue, even when the location of their coexistence has been the single mind of a great scientist or a great musician. Or, to take a more common example: In every daily newspaper across America today there was probably some notice of the time of "sunrise" and "sunset." In our culture, enamored and infused as it is with Western science, we know this is nonsense. The sun stands at the center of our planetary system; the earth moves around it. The sun cannot "rise" or "set." Yet there is meaning, and hence truth, for us in the expressions "sunrise" and "sunset"—poetic truth, romantic truth, spiritual truth. For this reason we have not found it necessary, or even desirable, to bring these perspectives into dialogue with our scientific perspectives. We nurture them both, in comfortable isolation from one another.

From the perspective of the scientific disciplines, things look a bit different. Religions are a datum of our world—our human, if not our material, world—and consequently scientists cannot completely ignore their presence. At minimum, the fields of sociology, psychology, business, education, political science,

> O ne of the most creative impulses of American culture is the continuing presence of religion at the heart of scientific civilization.
>
> —*James Gilbert*[11]

and philosophy, all of which rely on the scientific method, have *some* vested interest in coming to terms with religious truths. One could also make the case for biology and medicine, and for cosmology: the former because Western science now acknowledges a link between a person's physical health and his or her "spiritual" well-being; the latter because astronomers and cosmologists often demand a hearing from those who favor a theological solution to the mysteries of the universe.

In sum, it appears that certain disciplines of science are in need of a dialogue with religions, while most religions have no need at all for a dialogue

(a)

(b)

Science and Religions. (a) The "Space Window" at the National Cathedral in Washington, DC, is an attempt to bring religion and science together in a religious setting. In the middle panel of this stained glass window, above images of planets and stars and hovering over a cross, is a piece of lunar rock, donated by NASA. Displaying both the glories of God (the Creation) and the glories of man (scientific exploration), the window celebrates scientific accomplishments in the service of God. (b) The attempt to bring science and religion together in a "Christian science" in the late nineteenth century is the origin of the "reading rooms" that one finds in many American cities. (Will Deming) with the sciences. This is not to say, of course, that adherents of a particular religion will not find a dialogue with the sciences *desirable*. For social or political reasons, or for purely intellectual and theological reasons, a given tradition may well choose to pursue such interaction. Among the sciences, however, certain disciplines do not have this option.

If this is correct, the possibility emerges that the dialogue between science and religions has been misconceived, even by theologians. In the wake of Darwin, Einstein, and the rise of the social sciences, it has become a given among intellectuals in the West that religions must reconcile themselves to the claims of science. As we have just determined, however, this is not so. Instead, it is incumbent upon certain disciplines of science to come to terms with the claims of the world's religions. It is *they* who do not have the luxury of forgoing dialogue. By the same token, furthermore—and this may sound shocking to most Westerners—this dialogue will not be one of equal dialogue partners. Scientists cannot dismiss a religion as untrue in the way that a religious adherent can dismiss science as untrue. No scientist, using the methods and data of science, can claim that the Buddha did not achieve enlightenment, that Jesus is not the Son of God, or that Muhammad is not the prophet of Allah. These matters are simply beyond the purview of scientific inquiry. Religions, however, can and do brand the sciences as superficial or insubstantial, and this is well within their purview.

> Can a workable marriage between science and religion nonetheless be achieved that will allow our species to face the future with intelligence and inspired hope?
>
> —*John Avise*[12]

I conclude by suggesting that the prospects for a meaningful exchange between theologians and scientists will be helped considerably when scientists move from a position of questioning, exposing, and debunking religions to one of appreciation for the study of religion. To be truly *partners* in dialogue they must attempt some degree of empathy for the possibility of a reality beyond the physical world. To paraphrase Rudolf Otto: If a scientist has no appreciation for ultimate reality and no deference to those who have, he or she will do well to stay clear of this dialogue.

> Although the basic beliefs of religious systems are unacceptable, a purely destructive approach is at present inappropriate.
>
> —*Scientist Robert Hinde*[13]

NOTES

PREFACE

1. Wilfred Cantwell Smith, "Theology and the World's Religious History," in *Toward a Universal Theology of Religion*, ed. Leonard Swidler, (Orbis, 1987), 55.

CHAPTER 1

1. Statistical information in this book is based on David B. Barrett, George T. Kurian, and Todd M. Johnson, *World Christian Encyclopedia* (Oxford University Press, 2001), vol. 2, 3–12.

2. James C. Livingston, *Anatomy of the Sacred*, 5th ed. (Prentice Hall, 2005), 3.

3. Arnold Toynbee, *Change and Habit* (Oxford University Press, 1966), 184.

4. Wilfred Cantwell Smith, "Comparative Religion: Whither—and Why?," in *The History of Religions: Essays in Methodology*, ed. Mircea Eliade and Joseph M. Kitagawa, (University of Chicago Press, 1959), 44.

5. Ninian Smart, "Religion as a Discipline?," in *Concept and Empathy*, ed. Donald Wiebe (New York University Press. 1986), 162.

6. From a speech given to the American Israel Public Affairs Committee, April 23, 2002. (By contrast, United Nations Resolution 242 specifies an eventual Israeli withdrawal from "occupied territory.")

7. Bernard Lewis, *The Crisis of Islam* (Modern Library, 2003), xxviii–xxix.

8. Paul S. Boyer, "When U.S. Foreign Policy Meets Biblical Prophecy," 20 February 2003, ⟨http://www.alternet.org/story.html?StoryID=15221⟩ (accessed 31 March, 2003).

9. The dawning of a market research that takes account of religious preferences is indicated by the appearance of studies such as Philip M. Parker, *Religious Cultures of the World: A Statistical Reference* (Greenwood, 1997). There have also been important advances in the sociology of religion: See, for example, Rodney Stark and Roger Finke, *Acts of Faith: Explaining the Human Side of Religion* (University of California Press, 2000).

10. Jeppe Sinding Jensen, "What Sort of 'Reality' Is Religion?," in *Religious Transformations and Socio-Political Change*, ed. Luther Martin, (Mouton de Gruyter, 1993), 368.

11. Cited in Nancy Haught, "Sept. 11 Puts Islam Series in Sharper Focus," *The Oregonian*, November 24, 2001, B11.

12. Richard Rorty, "Cultural Politics and the Question of the Existence of God," in *Radical Interpretation in Religion*, ed. Nancy K. Frankenberry, (Cambridge University Press, 2002), 76.

13. Here are the actual beginning lines of an online BBC report for August 1, 2002: "Pope John Paul II has celebrated a mass for the beatification of two Mexican Indians, concluding a packed tour of the Americas. The ceremony mixed traditional Catholic elements with influences from the indigenous culture of the two Zapotec Indians, Juan Bautista and Jacinto de los Angeles. The two were lynched in 1700 after denouncing the pagan activities of their communities to the Catholic authorities. Their beatification is the last step before sainthood. After the ceremony, crowds gathered to see the Pope leave the Mexican capital to return to Rome, shouting 'Don't go! Don't go!' While the trip has been seen as a success, the 82 year-old pontiff—who suffers from Parkinson's disease and arthritis—was visibly frail, again fueling speculation about his health. One of the highlights of the tour was the canonisation of Mexico's first indigenous saint, Juan Diego, in a ceremony watched by hundreds of thousands. But the Pope looked extremely tired and struggled to keep his head up. At one point he was apparently asked by an aide if he wanted someone else to read for him." <http://news.bbc.co.uk/1/low/world/americas/2166970.stm> (accessed 6 July 2004).

14. Cited by Phil Kloer, Cox News Service, July, 13, 2002. Kloer himself gives this summary: "There have been nuns caught in windy updrafts ('The Flying Nun'), men in drag as nuns ('Nuns on the Run'), nuns who aren't really nuns ('Sister Act'), sex-crazed nuns ('The Devils'), and, only occasionally, a serious, complicated nun ('Dead Man Walking')."

15. David Letterman, *The Late Show with David Letterman*, September 17, 2001.

16. See Nancy T. Ammerman, "Waco, Federal Law Enforcement, and Scholars of Religion," in *Armageddon in Waco*, ed. Stuart A. Wright, (University of Chicago Press, 1995). On the nature of religious violence, see Gabriel A. Almond, R. Scott Appleby, and Emmanuel Sivan, *Strong Religion* (University of Chicago Press, 2003).

17. Nasra Hassan, "An Arsenal of Believers," *The New Yorker*, 77.36 (November 19, 2001):38.

CHAPTER 2

1. From the "Introduction" to Mark C. Taylor, ed., *Critical Terms for Religious Studies* (University of Chicago Press, 1998), 6.

2. Jeppe Sinding Jensen, "What Sort of 'Reality' Is Religion?", in *Religious Transformations and Socio-Political Change*, ed. Luther Martin (Mouton de Gruyter, 1993), 357.

3. Clifford Geertz, "Religion as a Cultural System," in *Anthropological Approaches to the Study of Religion*, ed. Michael Banton (London, 1966), 13.

4. Robert S. Ellwood, *Introducing Religion from Inside and Outside*, 3d ed. (Prentice Hall, 1993), 8.

CHAPTER 3

1. Peter L. Berger, *The Sacred Canopy* (Doubleday, 1967), 33.
2. Translated by Wendy Doniger, *Hindu Myths* (Penguin Books, 1975), 27–28.
3. David S. Noss, *A History of the World's Religions*, 8th ed. (Macmillan, 1990), 71.

CHAPTER 8

1. From a brochure entitled "Islam: A Message of Love, Peace, and Understanding," by Maryam Chaudhry.

CHAPTER 11

1. A. Eustace Haydon, "From Comparative Religion to History of Religions," *Journal of Religion* 26 (1922): 587.
2. Russell T. McCutcheon, "Critics Not Caretakers," in *Secular Theories on Religion*, ed. Tim Jensen and Mikael Rothstein, (Museum Tusculanum, 2000), 169.

CHAPTER 12

1. Mahatma Gandhi, *Young India: 1919–1922*, 2d ed. (Huebsch, 1924), 804.
2. Caroline Franks Davis, *The Evidential Force of Religious Experience* (Oxford University Press, 1989), 29.
3. Rita Gross, "Female God Language in a Jewish Context," in *Womanspirit Rising*, ed. Carol P. Christ and Judith Plaskow, (Harper and Row, 1979), 169.
4. Rudolf Otto, *The Idea of the Holy*, 2d ed. (Oxford University Press, 1950), 8.

CHAPTER 14

1. Bernard Lewis, *The Crisis of Islam* (Modern Library, 2003), 8.
2. Diana L. Eck, *A New Religious America* (HarperSanFrancisco, 2001), 370.
3. Toby Lester, "Oh, Gods!" *The Atlantic Monthly*, 289.2 (February 2002):37.
4. More popularly: What would Jesus do? (WWJD)—that is, "What should I *do*, based on what Jesus *did*?"

CHAPTER 15

1. Theodor H. Gaster, *The New Golden Bough: A New Abridgment of the Classic Work by Sir James George Frazer* (Criterion, 1959), 738.
2. Daniel Gold, *Aesthetics and Analysis in Writing on Religion* (University of California Press, 2003), 24–25.
3. Rodney Stark and William Sims Bainbridge, *A Theory of Religion* (Peter Lang, 1987; reprint, Rutgers University Press, 1996), 324.

4. Jonathan Z. Smith, *Imagining Religion* (University of Chicago Press, 1982), xi.

5. A classic example is Jonathan Z. Smith, "Religion, Religions, Religious," in *Critical Terms for Religious Studies*, ed. Mark C. Taylor (University of Chicago Press, 1998), 269–84. See also Russell T. McCutcheon, *Manufacturing Religion*, (Oxford University Press, 1997), 192–213.

CHAPTER 16

1. Ninian Smart, "Beyond Eliade: The Future of Theory in Religion," in *Concept and Empathy*, ed. Donald Wiebe (New York University Press, 1986), 136. See also his "Toward an Agreed Place for Religious Studies in Higher Education," in this same book, 167, where he observes: "The theory that all religions point to the same truth is a conclusion within a particular sort of dogmatic exploration. It is, for instance, typically expressed in modern Hinduism."

2. Wouter J. Hanegraaff, "New Age Religion," in *Religions in the Modern World*, ed. Linda Woodhead et al. (Routledge, 2002), 249–50.

3. William James, *The Varieties of Religious Experience* (Modern Library, 1902, and reprints), lectures XIV–XV, "The Value of Saintliness"—although James clearly saw the shortcomings of this approach.

4. Willard G. Oxtoby, *World Religions: Western Traditions*, 2d ed. (Oxford University Press, 2002), 507.

5. Catherine Bell, " 'The Chinese Believe in Spirits': Belief and Believing in the Study of Religion," in *Radical Interpretation in Religion*, ed. Nancy K. Frankenberry (Cambridge University Press, 2002), 110.

6. Frederick J. Streng, "Truth," in *The Encyclopedia of Religion*, vol. 15 (Macmillan, 1986): 72.

7. Stephen L. Carter, *The Culture of Disbelief* (Basic Books, 1993), 35.

8. Schubert M. Ogden, *Is There Only One True Religion, or Are There Many?* (Southern Methodist University Press, 1992), 13.

9. Martin E. Marty, *Sightings*, January 14, 2002 (an online publication of the Martin Marty Center at the University of Chicago Divinity School). ⟨http://martycenter.uchicago.edu/sightings/archive_2002/0114.shtml⟩ (accessed 30 April 2004).

CONCLUSION

1. Marsha Hewitt, "Reason Without Consolation," in *Secular Theories on Religion*, ed. Tim Jensen and Mikael Rothstein, (Museum Tusculanum, 2000), 33.

POSTSCRIPT

1. Sigmund Freud, *The Future of an Illusion*, trans. James Strachey (W.W. Norton, 1961), 56.

2. George A. Kennedy, *New Testament Interpretation through Rhetorical Criticism* (University of North Carolina Press, 1984), 157–158.

3. Arnold Toynbee, *Change and Habit* (Oxford University Press, 1966), 226.

4. Robert N. McCauley, "The Naturalness of Religion and the Unnaturalness of Science," in *Explanation and Cognition*, ed. Frank C. Keil and Robert A. Wilson (MIT Press, 2000), 82.

5. Blaise Pascal, *Pensées*, no. 423.

6. Albert Einstein, in his foreword to Homer W. Smith, *Man and His Gods* (Grosset and Dunlap, 1952, and reprints), ix.

7. From an interview with Charles Townes in W. Mark Richardson and Gordy Slack, *Faith in Science: Scientists Search for Truth*, (Routledge, 2001), 180.

8. Mircea Eliade, "History of Religions and a New Humanism," *History of Religions* 1 (1961): 5.

9. James Gilbert, *Redeeming Culture: American Religion in an Age of Science* (University of Chicago Press, 1997), 323.

10. Daniel Garber, "Religion and Science, Faith and Reason," *Criterion* 41 (2002): 38.

11. Gilbert, *Redeeming Culture*, 323.

12. John C. Avise, *The Genetic Gods* (Harvard University Press, 1998), 215.

13. Robert A. Hinde, *Why Gods Persist: A Scientific Approach to Religion* (Routledge, 1999), 233.

ANALYTICAL GLOSSARY OF RELIGIOUS TERMS

This glossary is offered as a catalyst for further reflection. By employing the categories of analysis outlined in this book, I have attempted to provide readers with suggestive examples of how they can think about religion and religions analytically. The terms included here are of two sorts: those used so commonly that their specifically religious meanings have been obscured (for example, "sacred") and those whose place in religious analysis is often overlooked. The phrase "higher realities" is used here as shorthand for higher-order realities *and* ultimate reality. An asterisk (*) after a word indicates that it has its own glossary entry.

agnostic: one who is uncertain as to the reality of higher realities.

androcentric religions: traditions in which males have readier access to ultimate reality than females.

angels, cherubs, demons, devils, ghosts, fairies, monsters, spirits, sprites: types of personified higher-order realities.

anthropomorphism: the envisioning of higher realities as beings with human attributes; a means of establishing common ground between profane and higher realities; rejected by some traditions as making ultimate reality too much like profane reality.

apologetics: the activity of making the symbols and inner-logic of one's own tradition intelligible to outsiders. See **propaganda***.

apostasy: the rejection of one symbolic system and vision of ultimate reality for another, opposing system.

asceticism: self-denial used as a tool for orientation; includes fasting, sleep deprivation, exposure to the elements, sexual abstinence, periods of **silence***. Compare **hallucinogens***.

astrology: the use of celestial phenomena as symbols in a religion or **quasi-religion*** (see **magic***, **spirituality***).

atheist: one who denies the reality of higher realities.

belief: see **faith***.

If you wish to be an intellectually interesting atheist, you are obliged to give some evidence for your position.

—Jim Holt

143

blasphemy: words or actions that powerfully disorient one from ultimate reality.

calendar: used by religions to orient adherents away from profane time, toward a more meaningful frame of reference. Religious calendars frequently impart meaning to profane time by establishing its beginning at a religiously significant point—for example, the birth of a founder (Christianity), God's Creation of the world (Judaism), or a prophetic act (Buddhism, Islam). See **time***.

ceremony, liturgy, rite, ritual: an ordered grouping of symbolic acts. See **worship***.

chaos: in some religions an awe-inspiring attribute of higher-order realities (as in demonic confusion, bedlam) or ultimate reality (as in divine madness or rage).

cleansing, purification: a process of orientation, usually mimicking hygienic cleansing, whose purpose is to counteract disorienting aspects of profane reality envisioned as "dirty" or "impure." These aspects often pertain to human mortality (illness, sexuality, procreation, blood, excrement, decay, death) and "moral filth" (**sin***, **evil***, violation). The agent of cleansing is sometimes anything but hygienic: polluted water, urine, cow dung, and blood.

community: orientation to ultimate reality via social relations, as in a "**holy*** community" over against "the world." In religious communities one's proximity to ultimate reality determines social hierarchy, and vice versa.

consecration: the act of orienting things or people to ultimate reality, often in such a manner that they must be kept apart from certain profane activities or contexts.

conversion: (1) becoming a partisan of a particular religion, often involving the repudiation of another; sometimes prerequisite for orientation to ultimate reality; (2) the orientation of outsiders; considered important by some but not all religions.

desert, wilderness, wasteland: envisioned as "buffer zones" between profane and higher realities; can be places of contact between these realities.

enlightenment: exceptional mental orientation to ultimate reality.

esoteric religion: religion kept secret from those not sufficiently oriented (outsiders, neophytes); employs secrecy as a symbol.

evil: a broad category of improper orientation to ultimate reality, including moral, physical, and spiritual disorientation. Compare to **sin***.

excommunication: a tradition's official denial to an adherent of the symbols necessary for orientation.

extremists, fanatics: those oriented to ultimate reality more fully than others find comfortable; those who are "very" oriented; often employing intolerance as a symbol. It should be noted that orientation to something *ultimate* logically tends toward extremism. Compare **omnipresence***.

faith: (1) orientation ranging from intellectual assent to all-encompassing devotion (as in a "man of great faith," or "faith in Christ"); (2) the worldview or **theology*** of a particular religion; often confused with **religion***, as in "the faiths of the world."

grace: orientation *by* higher realities *to* profane reality resulting in the latter achieving a better standing with the former.

hallucinogens: hallucinogens and other drugs are used as tools for achieving a level of consciousness more attuned to ultimate reality; includes peyote, hallucinogenic mushrooms, hemp, hashish, opium, wine, and tea (as an aid to maintaining focus in meditation). Other symbols used for this purpose include activities leading to physical exhaustion: bloodletting, fasting, sleep deprivation, exposure to the elements.

heaven, sky: often the geographical location of ultimate reality, envisioned as "infinite" or "ultimate" in height and breadth. See **location***.

heresy: orientation to ultimate reality wrongly conceived, or by means of the wrong symbols; a variation of a religious tradition founded on an incorrect vision of ultimate realty; the redefinition of the elements of a religious tradition that a majority of its adherents finds unacceptable. See **apostasy**.*

higher-order realities: superhuman beings, forces, and entities that are not ultimate; they stand between profane and ultimate reality (see **angels***, **magic***, **spirituality***).

holy, sacred: terms denoting a person or a thing's proximity to ultimate reality, and hence its usefulness as a symbol. For instance, a "holy book," a "holy relic," a "holy kiss." Also used in comparative and superlative expressions ("very holy," "most sacred," "holy of holies"); and of ultimate reality ("the sacred," "the holy one").

idol: an image used as a symbol (user's perspective); an image *mis*used as a symbol (polemical perspective).

idolatry: orientation to higher realities by means of images or points of reference deemed inappropriate by a religion's inner-logic.

laity: adherents who are not religious professionals—that is, not priests, clerics, monks and nuns, sages, or shamans. In most religions the laity's orientation to ultimate reality is inferior by comparison to that of its professionals.

legalism: a derogatory expression for religions that use laws as symbols.

location: often an important element of orientation. Ultimate reality or higher-order realities can be envisioned as "up there" (in heaven), "out there" (in a desert, forest, or outer space), "down there" (in an underworld), in the cardinal directions (especially east or west), or "at the center" (designated by a temple, a pole, an altar, or one's heart). Through location, orientation can take the form of physical orientation (toward the east or Mecca), physical movement (ascending a mountain, going on a **pilgrimage***), or spiritual movement (as in "turning inward").

magic: orientation to higher-order realities for the purpose of manipulating them; distinct, but not always separate, from religion. Used in religion as a symbol when orientation to ultimate reality necessitates controlling higher-order realities, as in Christian exorcism or Hindu and Buddhist tantric rituals.

martyrdom: accepting or inviting death as a means of orientation; to be distinguished from "suicide," which is a profane act that usually disorients one from ultimate reality.

mysticism: the most direct or intimate form of orientation to ultimate reality offered by a religious tradition; characterized by the immediate presence of (and sometimes union with) ultimate reality.

myth: in the study of religion, a nonhistorical narrative that conveys truths useful for orientation. Compare "epic," "legend," "sacred history," and "theological narrative," in which historical and nonhistorical truths are combined.

omnipresence, omnipotence, omniscience: characteristics of ultimate reality readily stemming from its ultimacy.

philosophy: intellectual inquiry into truth or reality, often relying on metaphysics; akin to **theology*** rather than **religion*** to the extent that the latter encompasses more than just intellectual or ethical orientation.

pilgrimage: a symbolic movement toward ultimate reality (and away from profane reality), conceived in terms of geographical movement (compare "spiritual retreat"). See **location***.

prayer: orientation by means of linguistic communication with ultimate reality; held to be necessary even when ultimate reality is omniscient.

prophecy: the announcement of information available only from higher realities; compare **revelation***.

quasi-religions: orientation to higher-order realities, but not ultimate reality; includes **magic***, **astrology***, extreme devotion to sports or hobbies, as well as some forms of **philosophy***, ethics, **spirituality***, witchcraft, and New Age religions.

reform, renewal, restoration: the attempt to orient oneself to ultimate reality by reviving earlier forms of a tradition; based on the conviction that a tradition's use over time in the context of profane reality has compromised its effectiveness.

religion versus religions: the former is an activity—orientation to ultimate reality (see chapter 2); the latter are symbolic systems ("traditions") that provide a means for such orientation.

revelation: a revealing or disclosure of higher realities.

sacrament: symbols that orient by dispensing important boons from higher realities; they usually require administration by religious professionals (see **laity***).

sacred: see **holy***.

saint: a person whose earthly life is oriented to ultimate reality to an exceptional degree; often one who is able to mediate between profane and ultimate reality. An instance of a person functioning as a symbol.

salvation: what religious adherents see as the result or reward of their orientation; sometimes synonymous with orientation itself, as orientation can be its own reward.

sanctuary, shrine, sacred precinct: a **location*** that provides special access to ultimate reality; often cordoned off from profane activities.

> It is of the essence of Absolute Reality that It is omnipresent.
>
> —*Arnold Toynbee*

> The errors in religion are dangerous; those in philosophy only ridiculous.
>
> —*David Hume*

> Realization of enlightenment (*satori*) is wonderful practice.
>
> —*Zen proverb*

scripture: writings deemed to be more closely oriented to ultimate reality than other literature (as in "**holy*** scripture"); writings especially conducive to orientation.

scripture interpretation, commentary: a means of keeping scripture viable as a symbol over time.

sexuality: (1) as sexual intercourse: a symbol in some **esoteric*** traditions (tantric Hinduism and Buddhism and esoteric Taoism); (2) as procreation: a cipher for a religious tradition's inner-logic, especially among agrarian and nomadic peoples.

shaman: a religious professional, usually in a tribal religion, who can mediate between profane, ultimate, and higher-order realities. Also "witch doctor," "priest," "medicine man." See **laity***.

silence: a negation of profane reality that offers space or opportunity for orientation to ultimate reality; one of many symbolic "wormholes" in profane reality.

sin: something that disrupts orientation to ultimate reality and for which humans may be held accountable. See **evil***.

spirituality: a sensitivity for and orientation to non-profane, "spiritual" realities, including (1) higher-order realities, (2) ultimate reality, or (3) both. In the first case, spirituality is a **quasi-religion***.

suffering: used as a creative opportunity for orientation, as human beings often reach out beyond profane reality in times of suffering.

symbol: a means for orientation to ultimate reality; see especially chapters 2 and 3.

talisman, fetish, amulet: symbolic tools for warding off or promoting interaction with higher-order realities; often unusual objects, indicating a point of reference beyond the profane world.

> Conceptualizations of what the sacred reality is are like symbols of the sacred within the mind.
>
> —*Robert Ellwood*

theology: the activity of reflecting on, articulating, and systematizing religion; more akin to **philosophy*** than **religion***; a tool for orientation by means of discursive thought.

time: invariable, plodding time is one of the attributes of profane reality. Profane time can be manipulated ("overcome") through symbols that orient one to "more real" time frames. Such symbols include sounds (from gongs, bells, drums), meditation, solitude, **pilgrimage***, ritualized behavior, and **calendars***.

ultimate reality: the focal point of religion and religions; see chapter 2.

wisdom: (1) discernment that depends on orientation to higher realities; (2) the insight into higher realities gained from such discernment. To be distinguished from **revelation*** and **prophecy*** (which do not necessitate discernment) and knowledge (which does not necessitate orientation).

worship: formalized activities for orientation; not synonymous with "**religion**"*. See **ceremony***.

Suggestions for Further Reading

HISTORICAL AND SYSTEMATIC OVERVIEWS
OF RELIGIOUS TRADITIONS

Coogan, Michael D., ed. *The Illustrated Guide to World Religions.* Oxford University Press, 1998.

Molloy, Michael. *Experiencing the World's Religions.* 3d ed. McGraw-Hill, 2005.

Nielsen, Niels C., Jr., Norvin Hein, Frank E. Reynolds, et al. *Religions of the World.* 3d ed. Bedford/St. Martin's, 1993.

Noss, David S. *A History of the World's Religions.* 11th ed. Prentice Hall, 2003.

Oxtoby, Willard G., ed. *World Religions.* 2 vols. 2d ed. Oxford University Press, 2002.

Schmidt, Roger, Gene C. Sager, Gerald T. Carney, et al. *Patterns of Religion.* Wadsworth, 1999.

OVERVIEWS THAT EMPHASIZE
CONTEMPORARY FORMS OF RELIGIOUS TRADITIONS

Esposito, John L., Darrell J. Fasching, and Todd Lewis. *World Religions Today.* Oxford University Press, 2002.

Fisher, Mary Pat. *Living Religions.* 5th ed. Prentice Hall, 2003.

Hinnells, John R., ed. *A New Handbook of Living Religions.* Blackwell, 1997.

Ridgeon, Lloyd, ed. *Major World Relgions: From Their Origins to the Present.* RoutledgeCurzon, 2003.

Woodhead, Linda, et al. *Religions in the Modern World.* Routledge, 2002.

Of special interest: Esposito, John L. *What Everyone Needs to Know About Islam.* Oxford University Press, 2002.

ANNOTATED SELECTIONS OF RELIGIOUS WRITINGS

Eliade, Mircea. *From Primitives to Zen: A Thematic Sourcebook of the History of Religions.* Harper and Row, 1967.

Fieser, James, and John Powers, eds. *Scriptures of the World's Religions.* 2d ed. McGraw-Hill, 2004.

Fisher, Mary Pat, and Lee W. Bailey, eds. *An Anthology of Living Religions.* Prentice Hall, 2000.

SPECIFIC TOPICS IN THE STUDY OF RELIGION

Bowker, John, ed. *The Oxford Dictionary of World Religions.* Oxford University Press, 1997.

Doniger, Wendy, ed. *Merriam-Webster's Encyclopedia of World Religions.* Merriam-Webster, 1999.

Eliade, Mircea, ed. *The Encyclopedia of Religion.* 16 vols. Macmillan, 1986.

Smith, Jonathan Z., ed. *The HarperCollins Dictionary of Religion.* HarperSanFrancisco, 1995.

Wuthnow, Robert, ed. *The Encyclopedia of Politics and Religion.* 2 vols. Congressional Quarterly Inc., 1998.

Young, Serinity, ed. *Encyclopedia of Women and World Religion.* 2 vols. Macmillan Reference USA, 1999.

DEMOGRAPHIC INFORMATION ON RELIGIONS

Barrett, David B., George T. Kurian, and Todd M. Johnson. *World Christian Encyclopedia: A Comparative Survey of Churches and Religions in the Modern World.* 2 vols. Oxford University Press, 2001.

HISTORIES OF THE STUDY OF RELIGION

Capps, Walter H. *Religious Studies: The Making of a Discipline.* Fortress, 1995.

———. *Ways of Understanding Religion.* Macmillan, 1972.

Hicks, David. *Ritual and Belief: Readings in the Anthropology of Religion.* 2d ed. McGraw-Hill, 2002.

Sharpe, Eric J. *Comparative Religion: A History.* 2d ed. Open Court, 1986.

Wiebe, Donald. "Religious Studies as a Saving Grace?" In *Religious Transformations and Socio-Political Change,* ed. Luther H. Martin. Mouton de Gruyter, 1993. 411–438.

THREE CLASSICS IN THE STUDY OF RELIGION

Berger, Peter L. *The Sacred Canopy.* Doubleday, 1967.

Eliade, Mircea. *Cosmos and History: The Myth of the Eternal Return.* Harper and Row, 1959.

James, William. *The Varieties of Religious Experience.* Modern Library, 1902, and reprints.

THEORY AND METHOD IN THE CURRENT STUDY OF RELIGION

Cunningham, Lawrence S., and John Kelsay. *The Sacred Quest*. 3d ed. Prentice Hall, 2002.

Ellwood, Robert S. *Introducing Religion: From Inside and Outside*. 3d ed. Prentice Hall, 1993.

Jensen, Tim, and Mikael Rothstein. *Secular Theories on Religion*. Museum Tusculanum, 2000.

Kessler, Gary E. *Studying Religion: An Introduction Through Cases*. McGraw-Hill, 2003.

Livingston, James C. *Anatomy of the Sacred*. 5th ed. Prentice Hall, 2005.

Platvoet, Jan G., and Arie L. Molendijk. *The Pragmatics of Defining Religion*. Brill, 1999.

Schmidt, Roger. *Exploring Religion*. 2d ed. Wadsworth, 1988.

Smart, Ninian. *Concept and Empathy*. Donald Wiebe, ed. New York University Press, 1986.

———. *Worldviews: Crosscultural Explorations of Human Beliefs*. 3d ed. Prentice Hall, 2000.

Taylor, Mark C., ed. *Critical Terms for Religious Study*. Chicago University Press, 1998.

RELIGIOUS PLURALISM IN AMERICA

Eck, Diana L. *A New Religious America*. HarperSanFrancisco, 2001.

Neusner, Jacob, ed. *World Religions in America: An Introduction*. Westminster/John Knox, 1994.

Tweed, Thomas A., and Stephen Prothero. *Asian Religions in America: A Documentary History*. Oxford University Press, 1999.

QUASI-RELIGIONS

Price, Joseph L., ed. *From Season to Season: Sport as Religion in America*. Mercer University Press, 2001.

Van Ness, Peter H., ed. *Spirituality and the Secular Quest* (World Spirituality vol. 22). Crossroad, 1996.

Other sources for the study of religion include specialized sites on the Internet and, naturally, religious people, groups, and organizations.

INDEX

Abdu'l-Baha, 74
Abortion, 6, 124
Abraham, 50, 52
Adonai, 51–52
Advertising, 132
Agnostic, 5
Ahmad, Mirza Ghulam, 74
Al-Aqsa Martyrs' Brigade, 7
Al-Qaeda, ix, 6
Ali, founder of Shiite Islam, 73
Allah, 7, 67, 68, 70, 71, 74, 104, 137
Almsgiving, 12, 67–68
Ambrose, Saint, 64
Ambry, 65
American flag, 16
Amida. *See* Amitabha
Amish, 19
Amitabha, 47
Analogies and images used in this
  book: ancient Chinese ritual for
  feeding ancestors, 96; botanist and
  gardner, 125–26; construction site,
  22, 102; consumerism, 95–96;
  financial news, 10; kiwi fruit,
  100–101, literary criticism, 88;
  market research, 95–96; religion as
  an ocean, 128; rocketship, 102–3;
  weightlifter, 39–40
Analysis of religion, 1, 9, 19–22,
  27–29, 93, 95, 103, 105, 128; ethics
  of, 104–5; as an ideology, 105;
  limits of, 100–103; neutrality in, 1,
  14, 105, 118, 126; and religious
  experience, 100–103; and religious
  language, 101; and religious
  tolerance, 118–26; stereotypes in,

10; versus participation in a religion,
  5, 9, 100, 102, 127–28
Ancestors, 26, 77, 96
Ancient Greeks, 129
Ancient Near East, 51
Ancient religions, 112
Androcentrism in religion, 90
Animal sacrifice. *See* Sacrifice
Animism, 76
Anthony, Saint, 64
Arabic, 72
Arjuna, 30
Ark, 55–56
Asceticism, 22, 30–31, 120
Atheist, 5
Atman, 35–36
Atom bomb, ix
Augustine, Saint, 88
Aum Shinrikyo, ix
Authority in religions, 54, 64–66, 68,
  70, 72–74, 90
Avalokitesvara, 46
Avatar, 29–30, 74
Avise, John, 137
Ayatollah Khomeini, ix, 74

Bab, 74
Baha'i, 74, 119
Baha'u'llah, 74
Bainbridge, William, 115
Bakker, Jim and Tammy, 10
Baptism, 14, 15, 59–60, 64, 95, 110
Bar mitzvah, 91
Bat mitzvah, 91–92
BBC, 139n13
Begin, Menachem, 7